THAT THEY
MAY BE MANY

THAT THEY
MAY BE MANY

*Voices of Women,
Echoes of God*

Ann Kirkus Wetherilt

CONTINUUM · NEW YORK

1994

The Continuum Publishing Company
370 Lexington Avenue, New York, NY 10017

Copyright © 1994 by Ann Kirkus Wetherilt

Printed in the United States of America

Library of Congress Cataloging-in-Publication Data

Wetherilt, Ann Kirkus.
    That they may be many : voices of women, echoes of God / Ann
Kirkus Wetherilt.
        p.   cm.
    Includes bibliographical references and index.
    ISBN 0-8264-0691-2 (alk. paper)
    1. Women in Christianity.   2. Feminist theology.   3. Revelation.
4. Pluralism.   5. Multiculturalism.   I. Title.
BV639.W7W46   1994
208.2–dc20   94–21312
                                                                CIP

Contents

Introduction

Monday, January 18, 1993. There is standing room only in New York City's Cathedral of St. John the Divine as hundreds gather to celebrate the life and mourn the death of Audre Lorde, the woman who had told them in words published, spoken, and lived that "my silences had not protected me. Your silence will not protect you."[1] The diversity of those assembled, and of the tributes and challenges offered, is testimony to the power of silences broken, of the truth of Lorde's claim that "it is not difference which immobilizes us, but silence."[2] The breaking of silence is at the heart of struggles for survival and liberation.

The Ase drummers and African-Caribbean rites, the poetry that exemplified the influence of a woman of powerful political and social conviction, the dance, the exuberance of the steel band, and the woman-respecting collect, reading, and benediction offered by the Reverend Renée Hill made manifest the power of "voices" when limitations are not placed upon modes of expression. Poet-activist Sonia Sánchez, one of many friends and family members to offer tribute to Lorde, embodied the diversity of voices as she moved from recitation to weeping, song to rejoicing, exhortation to keening. Audre Lorde's lifelong challenge to a single and reified "Word" of authority, whether proclaimed from podium, throne, or pulpit, was reflected in the celebrants' continuing call for coalition and commitment between and among women who are "Black and white, old and young, lesbian, bisexual, and heterosexual," who all share "a war against the tyrannies of silence."[3]

The chorus of multiple voices at Lorde's memorial celebration suggests a rich yet largely untapped resource for theo-ethical discourse.[4] The diverse peoples whose voices have not informed the white, Western, masculinist theo-ethical enterprise have been patronized, exploited, and even targeted for genocide by powerful "Christian" nations.[5] How might we develop a methodology through which the multiple voices of diverse cultures — and diverse people *within* cultures — could engage in theo-ethical dialogue with one another in the service of new possibilities for living together in the increasingly fragile world which we share? And how would such a methodology challenge the metaphors that have been central to historical Christianity?

In embarking on an exploration of such questions, any author must examine her or his own stakes in the project.[6] This does not eliminate the risks of co-optation or exclusion, but it can serve to acknowledge the privileged position of "author" of the text. In articulating my investment in my work, I try to hold myself accountable to my sources and to all those with whom I want to join in the creation of genuinely dialogic methods of engaging in theo-ethical discourse. For this same reason, I use the terms "we" and "our" throughout my text, rather than the more distanced constructions of a passive voice or the impersonal "one," to indicate both my own involvement in my work *and* my commitment to dialogue with any and all who might read these pages. Through the use of such terms, I assume no particular level of agreement with my suggestions and propositions, but rather a like commitment on the part of my readers to struggle with the deep questions of achieving greater quality of life for earth and all of its creatures, human and other, and particularly for those who have been most marginalized and exploited by the social systems that continue to dominate our local and global economic, political, and religious institutions.

The genesis of my interest in issues of language and knowledge, the multiple voices in which they are expressed, and their relationship to the revelation and activity of God in the world is, like most beginnings, multivalenced and complex. As a five-year-old, I hear my next-door neighbor tell her child that her skinned knee is "God's punishment" for her refusal to come when called. I ask my mother, "Is God like that?" We are not a church-going family. The minister comes to call occasionally, usually at meal times, and always with gossip about the sins of his parishioners, which my mother is undoubtedly supposed to apply to herself. It is not hard to imagine that the Reverend A works for the God who pushed Elizabeth down. But what about Canon B, gentle elder who guides me through my Anglican confirmation classes? Who is his God? Who is *my* God?

As a young child, I retreat into shyness as the "accent" acquired from my English mother masks the economic struggles of my family to "make ends meet" and labels me "uppity" among my schoolmates. I respond by frequent retreats into the world of books, and of sea and woods. I discover that knowledge — and God — is to be found in both places. Participating in antiapartheid demonstrations in the 1960s, against my New Zealand homeland's sporting connections with South

Africa, brings me to some awareness of the power of voices lifted in outrage and of the silencing of the voices of the Maori people in my country. Yet part of my "stake" is in reclaiming some of the integrity lost by the naive young teacher who thinks she is doing her Maori students an unambiguous favor by "helping" them to assimilate as anonymously as possible into the dominating culture.

Years and oceans away from New Zealand, I listen to a friend share tears and pain at her exclusion from the priesthood to which she feels called. The "inclusive words" I have advocated are not enough. As I intuited in my childhood, language goes deeper, into all of the structures and patterns of communication among a people. Changing the words no longer helps much when the images and symbols all tell me and my sisters that we can image God fully only when we shed our earthly bodies. I begin to seek new metaphors, plural and diverse, selected by those who need them in order to empower themselves to act in the world.

A variety of commitments, which cannot be separated into sacred and secular, personal and relational, theoretical and practical, challenges me in my work. Business as usual is not good enough. My own integrity demands that those experiences that are a direct part of my own life must enter into dialogue with the experiences of those with whom my life connects in less direct ways. As an academic, I acknowledge the particular power that I exert over my sources — all I can do is try to use this power responsibly, to claim only that authority that our past experiences and continuing conversations together will validate, as we struggle together for our own survival — that of our sisters and brothers, human and other-than-human, and of our planet.

I write from a feminist liberation perspective, aware that the voices of all women, and in particular those who are exploited economically and because of skin color, ethnicity, or sexual orientation, are still seldom heard in a definitive way in theological conversation in church or academy. Thus I am committed to a critical examination of all theological themes that serve the purpose of exclusion and marginalization. Because of my own social location as Christian, white, middle-class, highly educated, and relatively secure economically, I am concerned with the ways in which traditional theological concepts continue to maintain the privilege of those who share my own status and of those with still greater access to socially conferred power. I assume that, while I cannot speak for those from a cultural and social location different from my own, neither should I ignore their reality in my work. I acknowledge the epistemological privilege of works from persons whose racial/ethnic, class, gender, and sexual identities result in their domination by a coercive power elite.[7]

Much secular and theological feminist study has been undertaken around concepts of voice and language. In addition, religious feminists have begun to speak of the need for an authentic pluralism in the articulation of sacred experience and theo-ethical concepts. The endeavors of *both* of these projects are furthered by drawing connections between the metaphors used in Christian tradition and the potential of these metaphors for either empowering or silencing those who are not the "normative" human beings posited by white, Western, masculinist thought. The concept of "Word" has been invested with a particularly high degree of power and authority in Christian theological history, a history that is inextricably enmeshed in every society in which Christianity has formed a dominating part. The success of the religious political right in the United States in the late twentieth century is testimony to the impact such authority can exert beyond explicitly religious circles. The authoritative "Word" that is being spoken from the seats of theological and other power must be challenged if we are to hear the voices of those not conforming to the so-called normative definitions expressed by the representatives of powerful ecclesial and other institutions.

The Word — used by Christians to refer to scripture, to Jesus, or to God — has often functioned in empowering ways within particular Christian communities. But this same metaphor has all too often been used as a tool of control. Lesbian and gay persons in the United States and elsewhere have their basic rights to housing, jobs, and physical safety challenged daily by Christians appealing to a specific "Word" in the Bible. Those asserting the right and capacity of women to exercise agency in making their own reproductive choices are opposed by Christians who claim the "Word" of the church as Word of God. By claiming to be best qualified to expound the Word, church officials and their designated representatives arrogate to themselves the power to define and enforce the parameters of divine revelation. Any dissenting experiences, including those of marginalized peoples, are thus excluded from full and authentic participation in mainline ecclesial institutions. The "Word," a metaphor intrinsically suggesting expression, is distorted into a metaphor effecting silence.[8]

Christian theologians who would join the effort to dismantle the "tyrannies of silence" must both consider the implications of their own religious tradition and its doctrines *and* engage in the construction of new models for their theo-ethical explorations. Although my major focus in this study is on issues of race, class, gender, and sexuality, I acknowledge here that dialogue across the lines of religious traditions is a critical necessity in genuinely diverse theo-ethical discourse.

While it is critical for a feminist liberation theologian to acknowledge those dimensions of her own social location that are influential in determining the ways in which she relates in her everyday context, such naming in and of itself is not enough. It is equally important to engage the structures that perpetuate the exploitative dimensions of my "identity," particularly as these structures impede my movement into dialogue with women and others who do not share a given characteristic. In particular, I am concerned with challenging the boundaries that impose limits on dialogue and on mutual efforts to transform oppressive structures. At the same time, I insist upon the integrity of bonds of cultural and other affiliations.

Contemporary theological concerns are central to this study. Jesus claimed that "insofar as you did this to one of the least of these sisters and brothers of mine, you did it to me" (Matt. 25:40). The well-being of women, all women, is thus placed at the center of these theo-ethical explorations. A critical examination of historical and contemporary theological texts from a feminist perspective is always done with this commitment as central. The extent to which any text, metaphor, or normative theo-ethical demand enhances or diminishes the lives of women of any racial/ethnic, economic, or sexual background is a fundamental criterion for feminist claims of sacred revelation.

The voices that speak in this text are not exclusively those of women, and my intention is not to suggest that feminist theo-ethical discourse has nothing to learn from men or from continuing engagement with canonical scripture and other Christian tradition. Rather, in this work, the voices of *women* hold a privileged place. The lives of real, embodied women insofar as they can be known from the texts used here as resources, and the women who have been and are part of my many communities are a starting point for theoretical as well as experiential explorations. While not denying the continuing contributions to be made by traditional theological and other scholars, I choose as my primary sources women whose contemporary and historical struggles for survival and quality of life offer a resource to those committed to a similar endeavor in their *own* contexts.

Sources foreign to most theo-ethical texts in content, authorship, and mode of expression appear throughout this book. Autobiography and philosophy mingle with science fiction, other modes of imaginative fiction, poetry, and science. Feminist explorations in epistemology, literary criticism, and philosophy of science enter into dialogue with the creative expressions of women long denied any access to literacy or print, as well as those whose liberation struggles have yielded some level of participation in the world of the academy. Some cherished conceptions of identity politics are challenged for their possible polarizing effect, as well as affirmed for their nourishment of a sense of self among exploited groups. The experiences and expressions of many women, experiences and expressions ignored, deplored, or aborted by those manning the bastions of ecclesial and other pseudoholy power, provide glimpses of the divine reality that is beyond Word (or words) and that shines through in the treasured "sacred texts" that are primary resources for this study. This sacred presence, this incarnation of the holy, must not continue to be silenced through the unwillingness or assumed inability of persons from diverse communities and social locations to dialogue and work in coalition with one another in the day-by-day struggle for a more just and sane world.

This book does not presume to offer simple solutions as to how such demanding commitments can be either made or acted upon. Neither do I, as author, expect to have avoided the multiple pitfalls facing those who would seriously engage diverse voices. Given the pervasiveness of hegemonic mind-sets, the question must be not whether but to what extent the voices I have heard are my "own echo, a distortion of the original."[9] But perhaps even an echo can be a call for coalition and commitment in "a war against the tyrannies of silence."

Chapter 1

Power in Language
Laying the Groundwork for Inclusive Discourse

Changing a metaphor may not seem to be a necessary, much less a sufficient, solution to the problem of silence. Yet until we recognize the extent to which we are either betrayed or adequately represented by our language of immersion, we cannot know whether we have been silenced. A key component of the awareness of having been silenced is realization of the ways in which our language fails to express our own experience. Yet female churchgoers within mainline denominations offer an illustration of both the power *and* the inadequacy of linguistic patterns and changes. Women aware that something is wrong frequently believe that the substitution of inclusive language will correct the problem. Beginning by insisting that they do not feel included in language about "men" and "brothers," women may go on to challenge reference to God exclusively in male terms, since they too are supposed to be created in God's image. While women later recognize that such adjustments are only a first step, the resistance of church authorities to even this minor change indicates the power of language. Publication of the English translation of the new Universal Catechism of the Roman Catholic Church has been delayed because it is considered to be "too inclusive" in its language. And what is at stake in the catechism is not inclusive God-language, which is never attempted, but merely the replacement of terms such as "brethren." Both proponents and opponents of empowering the marginalized, then, have recognized the importance of language as an instrument that can be used for liberation or for repression.

In the current feminist movement, theorists have discovered the importance of language in empowering a community's capacity to live together in the world. Because language—broadly understood—is that through which all humans conceptualize their multifaceted experiences of living in the world, a brief examination of the insights of feminist theorists of language is in order.

Language: Toward More Adequate Definition

Language is central to all human experience; and particularly significant to the present study is its expression in diverse voices. Language both reflects and changes (or represses change in) social reality. Pamela Milne describes language as "one of the most distinctive features of our humanity" and points out that "language shapes us and we use language to shape our world.... With it we explore, we create and we influence the lives of others."[1] The centrality of language in defining as well as describing reality has led to a proliferation of texts on the subject by feminist theorists. In 1975, the publication of Robin Lakoff's *Language and Woman's Place* sparked debates about the existence of a particular style of writing and speaking developed by women in a sexist society.[2] Casey Miller and Kate Swift analyzed the impact of language on women's lives in social terms, focusing on the power of language both to liberate and to maintain current power structures.[3] Dale Spender examined the structure of the English language and concluded that the grammar, vocabulary, and syntax were "man-made" in their fundamental construction.[4] Mary Daly's *Beyond God the Father* moved the discussion into the specifically theological arena by challenging male language and metaphors not only for persons but also for God.[5] While more recent texts address critically what now appears to be an inadequate analysis of the complex phenomena that make up language patterns and discourse,[6] these early volumes have become classics in their fields because of their continuing capacity to raise consciousness about the consequences of linguistic sexism.[7]

When the language analyzed by Lakoff, Miller and Swift, Daly, and others has occurred in printed form, it has been granted an excessively privileged place. Even as I use and produce written text within these pages, I am conscious of the value of multiple forms and expressions of language. The fullness of human language goes beyond the words spoken by any and all cultural groups to include the multiplicity of "signs, sounds, gestures, marks and expressions" that any group employs to communicate among its members.[8] In a pluralistic world, where even many in the so-called first world are described as functionally illiterate, and communication with nonhuman species such as gorillas and dolphins is being explored, new understandings of language and communication are called for. The printed text alone is not adequate to the task of empowering conversations between diverse persons and even species.[9] The equation of language and authority with the printed text must be challenged. Language can and must be redefined in such a way that it includes all the means by which those who share this planet transmit and communicate their thoughts and feelings, information, and history. Language adequate to this task is contextual, relational, and dynamic.

Language as Contextual and Historical

Language neither emerges from nor flows out into a vacuum. Rather, language has its roots in the historical experiences of the people who use it, even as it continually shapes and names their particular social context. Discourse, which refers to the social nature of language, is the context in which our capacity to perceive ourselves as subjects is formed. Such discourse is never ideologically neutral but is rooted in the culture from which it emanates. Just as there is no such thing as a self that can be established apart from its social context, so is there no language system that does not embody in its very structures the ideologies and values of the power elite of the society in which it develops.[10] What is still regarded in most academic circles as normative, acceptable "English" is no exception. Language, like the annals of history, reflects the reality of those who have achieved and retained power over the dominating naming and meaning-producing activities of the society.

Yet dominant language and meaning are not *all* that exists. Communities of struggle have long known the coming to voice that occurs when they rediscover their own "subjugated knowledges."[11] Feminist theologian Sharon Welch has discussed how these knowledges "refer to a specific history, the history of subjugation, conflict, and domination, lost in an all-encompassing theoretical framework or erased in a triumphal history of ideas."[12] A community's history of domination and subjugation, however, does not constitute the totality of that community. While recovery and analysis of this history are essential to the community's liberation struggle, a large part of the group's capacity for survival is the symbolic and mythic culture and language that have been kept alive through diverse means of expression — through the people's retention of "voice."

If social and historical context is vital for understanding the development of particular expressions of a people, equally important are the contextual nature of words themselves and the other components of language-exchange. Such an understanding of language is embodied in a so-called obsolete definition of *context* as "the weaving together of words in language."[13] Most white, Western Christian theologies have lost this particular definition and have instead tended to focus on sacred power as a spiritualized, isolated "Word" increasingly removed from the context of human "language." This trend is most evident in extreme manifestations of Protestant biblicism and Roman Catholic magisterialism, where the Bible and the church, respectively, function to control the beliefs and actions of persons in the name of a God who is seen as represented most fully in our time in the pages of scripture or in the pronouncements of the Roman magisterium.

The distancing of sacred reality and revelation from the lived context of communities of faith is a strange phenomenon in a religious tradition founded on belief in incarnation. If Christianity has anything of value to offer to a world in danger of total ecological and/or nuclear destruction, it is in its affirmation of sacred presence in and among physical realities, including but not limited to all human persons. This affirmation does not deny the *transcendence* of the divine, when transcendence is understood in its root sense of "crossing over." If incarnation implies the "crossing over" of the boundaries between human and divine, then these two facets of Christian belief are integral to one another. Tom Driver suggests:

> All organisms transcend their environment precisely by their immersion in it — that is, to the degree that they *act* in it. Their acting is a measure of their engagement. If the human environment is vaster and more complex than that of an orange tree, it means that the human is more deeply engaged with the environment — by virtue of eyes, ears, ambulating limbs, and so on, including imagination. Far from being free of the environment, humans are free in it, to it, and with it, provided only that they recognize how they and their environment coinhere. Awareness of this seems to me the authentic motive for scientific inquiry.[14]

An understanding of words and language as inherently contextual and historical can enable us to assess critically appeals to a "transcendent," distant deity whose relationship with "his" people must be mediated through allegedly objective dominant language by "his" representatives. Creative resistance to dominating structures requires insistence upon the possibility of revelation through a multitude of diverse expressions by incarnate beings.

Language as Relational

The need and desire of all persons to communicate with one another are primary motivations for the acquisition of language. Even the most isolated scholar locked in an office, a study, or a monastery cell has presumably written in order to communicate something to someone. Indeed, words must be read and/or heard and recognized before they even exist as words.[15] Language in its many forms is our way of expressing and deepening our diverse connections with one another. In the exchange of language in conversation, both listener and speaker play interdependent roles. Nelle Morton describes her own deepened awareness of the significance of the role of listener as she hears a woman describe the ways in which she had been empowered to discover her own voice:

> This woman was saying, and I had experienced, a depth hearing that takes place before the speaking — a hearing that is far more than acute listening. A hearing engaged in by the whole body that evokes speech — a new speech — a new creation. The woman had been *heard* to her own speech.[16]

The listening that Morton describes goes far beyond mere reception of the words spoken. This "depth hearing" gives evidence to the one speaking that the experiences to which she gives voice are significant and are valued by the one to whom she speaks. The act of listening deeply may be related to what is often referred to as "women's intuition." One of the women interviewed by Dale Spender makes this connection in noting, "Women aren't blessed with intuition. They just listen in a way that men don't, right? . . . When you're *just* listening, you pick up all kinds of information. And when you *act* on it, you know, that's when people say how *intuitive* you are!"[17]

What has been seen as problematic with women's language, making such language "ineffective" in terms of traditional masculinist discourse, may be related more to women's commitments to keeping the lines of communication and thus relationality open than to uncertainty and lack of self-confidence. The oft-noted use of tag questions is a case in point. The inclusion of such questions as "isn't it?" or "don't you think?" at the end of statements of opinion is not necessarily an indication of weakness or lack of assertiveness, but rather may be an invitation to the listener to add her or his perspective to what the speaker sees as a dialogue, not a pronouncement.[18]

Language as Dynamic

Language is dynamic both in its structures and in its expressions. By "dynamic," I mean that language patterns are not static and fixed, that they retain a certain flexibility that enables them to change as required to reflect shifts in meaning within the cultures in which they are embedded. A word such as "awful" has shifted in meaning from "able to inspire awe" to something distasteful that should be avoided; "byte" has entered the common vocabulary, a product of the computer age. This does not deny the need for a certain continuity and stability in any language that is to serve a community as a medium of communication over time. Rather, a focus on the dynamism of language enables one to see that if its oppressive and exclusionary patterns were man-made and have changed over time, they are not "natural" and thus can be re-created.[19]

Historically, the task of lexicographers and their forebears has been one of articulating the relationship between words and their meanings. With the advent of dictionaries and grammars, this process was formalized in a medium that concretized language in a stable form. As with all forms of printed matter, questions must be asked as to who had access to the techniques of dictionary-making and whose language was encoded within the pages of the resulting volumes. Referring to the "socio-political aspects of dictionary-making," Deborah Cameron suggests that the very structure of a dictionary tends to obscure the ways in which language patterns develop and change, and at best can only hint at the complexity involved.[20]

This power of language, to change both in its own expressions and structures and in its capacity to shift perceptions of the experiences of the culture in which it is situated, is of critical importance to any attempt to broaden spheres of discourse to incorporate long-excluded perspectives and expressions of knowledge. Language, including its symbols, metaphors, images, and diverse articulations, is a powerful force at work both in protecting existing power structures from change and in empowering subjugated peoples and groups in retaining their own sense of dignity and in struggling together for justice. What are some of the ways in which diverse peoples come to full articulation of their own voices, and how might these voices *in*form and *trans*form theo-ethical discourse? Privileging a concept of "voices" rather than that of "Word" provides us with a metaphor more adequate to the task of moving beyond an excessive association of communication with printed text and encourages a greater appreciation of the dynamism and diversity of multiple expressions of sacred revelation.

While institutionalized religious traditions often have been adopted in empowering ways by communities of struggle, they have also served to legitimate existing structures of domination and thus to hold them in place. The ways in which religiously imbued symbols and metaphors achieve a powerful life of their own increase both the danger and the life-enhancing potential of the images in question. Demands for obedience to the "Word" of ecclesial authority exemplify the power of such a metaphor as it has become entrenched in Roman Catholic tradition; scripture as literal "Word of God" fulfills a similar function in Protestant biblicism. Although such habitual obedience cannot be eliminated by theory, persons can achieve a degree of personal and communal liberation through critical exploration of new understandings of deeply cherished beliefs.

The many manifestations of language exert a great deal of power in the construction and expression of the life of any community. Attention must also be given to the unequal relationships of power that inhere both within and among communities of human and other-than-human entities. Yet dialogue across the lines of socially imposed and controlled differences is vital in a world where the connections between multiple expressions of exploitation are increasingly clear. This dialogue is fraught with the danger of co-optation and misunderstanding, hostility and paternalism. Any theo-ethical project that promotes such dialogue must pay careful attention to the criteria used to both select and make use of materials issuing from a community or group to which the author stands in a power-differentiated relationship. Although power relationships are seldom if ever uni-dimensional, I focus here on criteria that apply to those who stand in a relationship of socially endowed privilege to the communities from which the resources emerge.

Criteria for Selection and Use of Sources

The construction of criteria for the selection and use of sources raises many questions for those theo-ethicists like myself who are committed to doing theological work that enhances rather than diminishes our capacities for living together with dignity on this earth we share. As a lesbian woman, I have long been alert to the mal-appropriation, by men and sometimes other women, of texts and realities from my own experience. As a white woman raised in New Zealand, my increasing knowledge and experience of racist history and contemporary practice in the United States have evoked a sense of embarrassment and shame at my own and my people's devastating ignorance of our history of colonization and abuse of the indigenous Maori peoples. With Minnie Bruce

Pratt, I say that "I'm trying to get a little closer to the longed-for but unrealized world, where we each are able to live, but not by . . . someone else's blood or pain."[21]

No particular experience may be used to posit universal theory. But this acknowledgment need neither prohibit the development of theory at all nor deny any use of insights from cultures and experiences other than those in which we are personally immersed.[22] The tensions inherent in the complex task of taking seriously the experiences and voices from multiple individuals and communities, variously situated in terms of their power relationships with each other, cannot and should not be minimized. In our awareness of these tensions, however, lies the possibility of avoiding simplistic misappropriation and of taking the risks necessary for engaging in dialogue that will sometimes be fraught with anger and mistrust. Criteria, methodologies, and strategies must be developed that can enable evaluation of the integrity with which any of us approaches the sources and resources developed in the context of communities with whom we stand in "power-differentiated" relationships. Although I speak here predominantly of women's experiences, I suggest that similar criteria might be effective for many others, including men, who would enter into dialogue across lines of socially imposed differences. In the current political climate, our survival and that of the planet itself depend on our discovering ways to work together across the lines that are set up to keep us divided and alienated.

Any discussion of criteria or theo-ethical method needs to include the issue of power. Few terms have been as much used and as inadequately explored and understood in white feminist work as "power." Although a variety of forms and/or dimensions of power are at work in any relationship, under consideration here are those structured, institutional power dynamics that uphold race, class, and gender/sex exploitation, and the difference such dynamics make in attempts to work together across lines of difference. Virginia Harris and Trinity Ordoña clarify one of the distinctions I am making here. "Racism is prejudice *plus* power — control of others' lives, power over. Cross-racial hostility is prejudice *plus* trying to *feel* powerful. Very different!"[23]

On the other hand, there is "power" in a positive sense. We speak of the power of a particularly moving piece of music, of poetry, and of other art forms. Some of us have known the power in the roar of ocean waves and in the quiet beauty of winter woods. We have been *em*powered by friends and communities who have stood with us through difficult times. We experience enabling and transformative power when we live and move with one another to exercise our collective and individual agency in the world. This power underlies my assertion that the sacred is indeed revealed in struggles for greater justice and dignity.

Even in framing the terms and method of this book, I experience power dynamics in various ways. On the one hand, I acknowledge the multiple "privileges" that enabled me to embark on extended graduate education. Yet I affirm also the ways in which I overcame many of my own self-doubts, with the empowering assistance of many friends, to move in this direction. I experience a certain powerlessness in that what I write is assessed by those with power to grant or withhold publication, yet inevitably I exercise power in comparable ways over the sources that I incorporate into my work.[24] The criteria suggested below are intended to offer a starting point for all of us who would attempt authentic dialogue across lines drawn to separate and who are conscious of the multiple and sometimes contradictory power dynamics that work among and between us.[25]

Differences, Not Otherness

If the relationships that exist between any person and another group or individual are acknowledged, in both their oppressive and life-enhancing dimensions, then those communities and persons cannot be seen as totally "other." The *use* of work from "different" communities must be grounded in respect for the integrity of both community and resource *and* in consciousness of the ways in which the work relates to our own. Judith Plaskow speaks of the ways in which false assumptions of a common "Judeo-Christian tradition" have the effect of "effacing an independent Judaism."[26] Yet Plaskow insists also that the ways in which our experiences *do* converge must be acknowledged.

"Difference" has become a major category of analysis in contemporary theoretical work in many disciplines. If this concept is to be useful in practice and not just in theory, we must talk about "differences" in the plural. By this means, we can take seriously the multiple differences that exist within and among diverse communities and individuals. María Lugones suggests that white feminists tend to recognize the *problem* of difference without recognizing differences themselves.[27] Using the image of a "boomerang gaze," which allows white women to look at the "other" and see only a mirror image of their own concerns reflected back,[28] Lugones insists that many white women thus assume that the "problem" of difference is with universalized *theory* rather than with the embodied relationships among differently situated women.

A "theorizing" of difference that leaves unjust social relationships intact does nothing to enhance genuine interaction and resists attention to the fact that differences due to racism, for example, cannot be understood in the same way as those due to imperialism or colonialism. In addition, this theoretical approach tends toward the "noninteractive acknowledgment" that can allow one to pay lip service to differences while avoiding authentic engagement.[29] Understanding differences as embodied in the real lives of diverse women precludes simple conceptions of identity. It also mitigates against an abstract concept of "difference" that is not grounded in the reality of people attempting to converse across the boundaries formed by the structuring of rigid identity.

Abstract notions of "difference" and "otherness" frequently have replaced an appreciation of embodied differences in the work of well-meaning white feminists. Liberal white women have tended, for example, to invite in an African-American woman to talk only about racism. While we cannot engage authentically the works of racially diverse women without attention to questions of racism, reduction of the voice and expertise of African-American women to the issue of race is but a form of tokenism.

Also at stake here is the need to acknowledge the differences that exist *within* any given community. If traditional scholarship's practice of subsuming women's experience under the so-called generic "man," or even "human," has taught feminist scholars anything, it should be an awareness of the inadequacy of universalizing terms of description. Yet even when feminist language demonstrates a consciousness that "women's experience" is overly universalizing, one frequently hears such terms as "Asian women," "white women," "the African-American community," and the still more problematic "women of color." Issues such as economic status, sexual orientation, and level of formal education, to name only a few, make for dramatically different perceptions within any specific group.

In addition, there is a need to resist the temptation to "specialize" a particular individual or group as those with whom we want to dialogue. This "specialization" can take the form of choosing to speak with those who are least likely to unsettle one's own comfort level and/or of romanticizing "difference" in the cultural reality of the "other." Trinh Minh-Ha outlines the imperialistic consequences of this stance:

> Specialness as a soporific soothes, anaesthetizes my sense of justice;
> it is, to the wo/man of ambition, as effective a drug of psychological self-intoxication as alcohol is to the exiles of society. Now, i
> am not only given the permission to open up and talk, i am also
> encouraged to express my difference. My audience expects and demands it; otherwise people would feel as if they have been cheated:

We did not come to hear a Third World member speak about the First (?) World, We came to listen to that voice of difference likely to bring us *what we can't have* and to divert us from the monotony of sameness.[30]

As well as preselecting just which voices from any community will be included in what remains a conversation defined by the dominating group, such an approach also runs the risk of "replicating Eurocentric fascination with the exotic."[31] This not only gives a limited perspective on a complex cultural reality but also perpetuates the practice of failing to take differences seriously in their power-differentiated effects in women's lives by romanticizing an exotic "other."

Finally, sources and resources from another cultural reality and experience must be taken seriously enough for those who would be in dialogue to raise questions and engage the material critically. The experiences that inform these sources are frequently those of devastating histories and personal encounters of exploitation and struggle, not the least of which is sometimes the struggle for basic literacy and the ability to appear in print. The sharing of such a resource is not for the purpose of *anyone's* enjoyment. Kwok Pui-Lan has articulated clearly the trivialization that occurs when the recounting of painful and challenging experiences is greeted with, "Thank you for your wonderful presentation. I enjoyed it so much."[32] There is no way to engage passionately and with integrity the experience of *any* other(s) without a willingness to question and explore that which we don't understand or with which we do not agree. Clearly, such questioning is rooted in a commitment to self-education and must move in the direction of all participants coming to a new understanding of their own relationship to the subject under discussion. But question and engage we must, if we are to move to greater understanding of the ways in which we can find common cause in our efforts to overcome all forms of domination and exploitation.

Passion

Passion has such diverse connotations that it may appear to be a term too laden with confusion to be useful here. Christians are familiar with the "passion of Christ," referring to Jesus' suffering in the events leading up to and including his ultimate death on the cross. At the other extreme, we talk of "unbridled passion," usually referring to sexual feelings that are out of control. My use of the term as a criterion for engagement of diverse sources incorporates dimensions of each of those definitions but goes beyond a synthesis of the two. One of the dictionary definitions of "suffer," which comes from the same root as "passion," is "to feel keenly."[33] The Christian focus on the physical abuse and violation of Jesus' body as defining his "passion" misses the ways in which he felt keenly during the other events of his life as they are reported in the Christian scriptures. His grief over Lazarus, his capacity for joy and celebration exemplified in the water-to-wine story of Cana, and his rage at the money changers in the temple are all manifestations of his "passion" — a keenly felt commitment to fullness of life.

The sources that are "primary" in this study are texts that evoke that sense of passion. Because I do not claim to be engaged in an "objective" project in which I maintain personal distance from my materials, I recognize but do not apologize for the personal bias present in determining which sources offer a sense of "passion." I have chosen books and other materials that have evoked passion in *me:* sometimes joy, sometimes rage, sometimes deep grief.

If passion is central in the selection of sources, it is also a critical dimension of the use made of the materials. The passion that leads to text selection is what empowers engagement with that text in ways that transform the ideas, commitments, and passions of the reader. Where there is *no* passion in a theo-ethical narrative that incorporates the voices of those whose very survival is testimony to their own passionate living, such narrative has not encountered the texts in authentic engagement. Carter Heyward claims:

> Our passion as lovers is that which fuels both our rage at injustice — including that which is done to us — and our compassion, or empathy with those who violate us, hurt us, and would even destroy us. Rage and compassion, far from being mutually exclusive, belong together. Each is an aspect of our integrity, for just as our rage is appropriate to our experience of lovelessness in the world, so too is our compassion the on-going acknowledgment and confession of our own refusals to make love in the world — beginning in our own homes, in our own beds, at our own altars.[34]

This link between passion, including its dimensions of rage, and *com*passion is too seldom seen. Christian compassion is often promoted as requiring premature easy grace in the form of a pseudolove that does not require the restoration or achievement of justice. Theological constructs that focus on easy reconciliation and forgiveness, without taking seriously the fury that oppression *should* evoke in healthy people, cannot be held to be salvific. Clearly, Heyward is aware that rage and compassion go together, or both are distorted beyond usefulness.

This is not to say that raw fury is in and of itself transformative of destructive structures. Audre Lorde affirms the "well-stocked arsenal of anger" that every woman has as a potential "source of energy serving progress and change." Yet Lorde also knows from experience that, even when the motivating factor for the rage is a racist remark, if fear of speaking turns the anger into silent resentment, "[T]hat unexpressed anger lies within...like an undetonated device, usually to be hurled at the first Woman of Color who talks about racism."[35] The affirmation of anger, or any other emotion, does not imply uncritical acceptance of any and every expression of that feeling. Beverly Harrison, too, affirms anger as "a vivid form of caring," a "feeling-signal" that can be trusted to let us know that "all is not well," and Harrison reiterates Lorde's caution that anger, like all feelings, is subject to ethical decisions in terms of how it will be acted upon.[36]

Heyward, Lorde, and Harrison all speak of passion, anger, love, and *com*passion in the same breath. All are profoundly embodied realities. It is this kind of "passion" that must inform all of our work for justice, including our academic theo-ethical discourse. This is the passionate commitment that can sustain us in the long haul because it knows that disappointments, conflicts, and pain will be accompanied by joy, humor, and celebration. A passionately embodied sense of commitment runs less risk of once again objectifying those with whom we hope to engage because it does not allow the kind of distance that can make an academic exercise of our work.

Responsibility/Relationship

Although all relationships imply a certain responsibility, and responsibility and accountability imply relationship, they must be held in particularly close proximity in any consideration of sources from a culture or other experience with which we stand in a relationship of inequality. The sources I have selected emanate from communities with which I experience some level of relationship, and thus responsibility. As one who has chosen to live in the United States, for example, I am through that decision "in relationship" with the people of Rigoberta Menchú, who are exploited and violated by U.S. economic interests and by U.S. support of repressive Guatemalan governments. Where my relationship with the authors of the texts is through similarity of the "privilege" of white skin and/or economic security, I assess the relevance of the work for my project in terms of demonstrated awareness of the unearned nature of that privilege and efforts to dismantle it.

My white skin ensures that my relationship with white feminist theologians is different from that with womanist and mujerista theologians, and there are specific accountabilities in each case. I am accountable with my white feminist sisters for my participation in our efforts to refuse the unearned rewards to which our white skin "entitles" us and to continue our analysis and challenges of the ways in which the systems in which we participate generate and support this privilege. With my womanist and mujerista sisters, I am responsible for informing myself of the historical and contemporary institutionalization of racism in socio-political structures and in my own mind. Judit Moschkovich issues a challenge:

> Don't speak about someone/something unless you can admit your ignorance on the subject. . . . I do not hold any individual American woman responsible for the roots of this ignorance about other cultures; it is encouraged and supported by the American educational and political system, and by the American media. I do hold every woman responsible for the *transformation* of this ignorance.[37]

There is a certain freedom to be gained in taking seriously Moschkovich's words, in that the weight of responsibility for all the evils of racist culture is not our personal burden. Yet along with such freedom comes the challenge of accountability. Early texts in feminist theology, written by white women, focused almost exclusively on issues of gender. We can no longer consider this an adequate emphasis when it is uninformed by analyses of race and class oppression. Walking through almost any section of New York City offers a graphic illustration of the reality that it is not true now, and never was, that we who have named ourselves — or have been named — normative in terms of cultural identity are in the majority in the world and that others are thus different from *us*. Neither can we ignore the constant reminders that those who are homeless are more likely to have skin darker than our own, just as those with whom we share academic and other institutional and cultural settings probably do not. The continuing challenge is what to *do* with our knowledge.

Part of the challenge of entering into authentic conversation with those who are different from us in one or another major dimension of social location is that of owning and claiming our own culture and history in all of its complexity. In her reflection on "identity," Minnie Bruce Pratt speaks of attempts to "leave our culture behind, disassociate ourselves from it."[38] Cutting ourselves off from our own historical situation is a particular form of *ir*responsibility that leads frequently to the "theft" of others' cultural practices to fill the gap and sense of rootlessness that this disconnection leaves in its wake. Pratt reflects on the ways in which she is aware of "using Black people to weep for me," particularly as she has come to awareness of something lost by her own white heritage through the structures of domination and imperialism. We need only consider the ways in which American Indian spirituality is misappropriated by white North Americans who "identify" with certain select dimensions of the culture. This identification occurs frequently in the absence of any awareness of a responsibility to examine the historical and contemporary relationship of Euro-Americans to the experience of genocide and exploitation of American Indian nations or of the context in which indigenous spiritual practices are authentically undertaken.[39] Kwok Pui-Lan warns:

> Religious symbols, sacred stories, great novels and literature emerge from peoples' yearnings, struggles, and visions. There is a holy dimension in them, because they illuminate the meaning of existence and the destiny of a people. If we take them out of context, we not only do injustice to the stories and symbols, but we also violate the integrity of the people.[40]

Part of the solution to such co-optation on the part of the privileged is recovery of our own submerged yet still-present tradition of persons who struggle against dominating and oppressive realities.

White women (and men) must then claim their very "whiteness" as a social characteristic that has placed them historically in varying relationships with persons of other ethnic and racial backgrounds. As those who are white approach the resources and experiences of multiethnic groups, it must be with an attitude of mature responsibility for their own ignorance, education, and action. Such an attitude acknowledges the distinction between shame and blame for past sins and accountability for present and future actions.

Beyond Identity to Praxis

In positing a need to move from a focus on "identity" to one on praxis, I acknowledge that a sense of group identity is easier to eschew when one has had that identity affirmed in the cultural milieu in which one lives. Because I give specific attention below to the tensions between group identity and the navigating of differences within any "identity," I simply acknowledge here the danger of a sense of identity as a fixed and static reality when approaching texts and other resources from those who are defined in terms of specific social location or characteristics. The need to categorize "others" in neat and orderly systems must be rejected in a liberative theo-ethical methodology that acknowledges differences within any given category as well as among them. Patricia Hill

Collins discusses the ways in which "additive models of oppression" are rooted in theories of identity:

> One must be either Black or white in such thought systems —
> persons of ambiguous racial and ethnic identity constantly battle
> with questions such as "what are you, anyway?" This emphasis on
> quantification and categorization occurs in conjunction with the
> belief that either/or categories must be ranked.[41]

Because of the ambiguous and multiple character of any individual's "identity" and the dangerous consequences of its use and abuse as a category of analysis, an emphasis on praxis is more likely to engender creative and constructive dialogue across lines of difference than is endless grappling with questions of identity. In the first instance, this may entail a commitment to engage in antiracist practices instead of proclaiming oneself to *be* a nonracist. This commitment implies a willingness to face the hostility and suspicion of those who have no reason to believe that they can trust our intentions. In Susan Thistlethwaite's *Sex, Race, and God,* the author quotes Ada María Isasi-Díaz as stating that "she had learned to trust white women who would 'cover your back.' "[42] Centuries of all-too-valid reasons for mistrust will not and should not be forgotten overnight. Covering one another's backs — a praxis of authentic solidarity — means moving beyond the fear that paralyzes us into taking "traitorous" stands that may leave us outside of the circle of affirmation of those we have called "our people."[43]

Transformation of Theological Method

If the criteria outlined above are to be taken seriously, the greatest challenge facing white feminist academic theologians is to develop a radical willingness to have their theological method uprooted and transformed by the new insights gained from authentic conversation with those who have been seen as "other." Efforts toward inclusion are merely token gestures when academic practices are not themselves modified to reflect the significance of race and class dynamics.[44] Ada María Isasi-Díaz suggests three components of a methodology through which resources from diverse cultures might be approached with integrity. First must come an effort to enter into the work, to understand it from the inside. Second, the work must be valued as important in its own right and not evaluated "according to how much we can use it." Finally, the work must confront, question, and challenge our own in such a way that a creative dialogue can take place, a dialogue that "thrives on tension, on difference; that...is not circular and that, therefore,...will lead us to a new place."[45]

The degree of openness to continuing transformation of the very methods of theorizing and engaging in the multiple modes of theo-ethical discourse determines the efficacy of any commitment to engage in authentic praxis. This must be the test of the seriousness of such commitment. Do we "welcome having those who were previously silent wrest our theory from us, altering and transforming it through their unique appropriation"?[46] Without this "welcoming" approach to our methodology, we cannot move beyond the ineffectualness of liberal goodwill into authentic engagement.

These criteria are but a beginning point. As I read and reread my own text, I discover the many ways in which my words do not always reflect my commitments. In continuing discussions with others, these criteria will be reviewed, revised, transformed, even discarded, according to their capacity to empower creative, justice-seeking discourse among diverse communities.

Language — which includes the symbolic and nonverbal expressions and communications developed by diverse human and other-than-human beings to relate with one another and understand their universe — is central to each of these criteria and to any attempt to achieve more just relationships among diverse persons. The ways in which we "speak" and listen to another's "speech" both affect and are affected by our own socio-historical location and commitments. Changes in language in and of themselves will not change oppressive structures and relationships, but consciousness of the power of language is a critical component in such change. Our Christian heritage, no less than the other social and political institutions within which it and we have interacted, has both empowered and distorted our efforts to engage diverse others in authentic discourse. It is past time for the authoritarian "Word" to be unseated and for a plurality of voices to be recognized as more expressive of the struggle to keep the sacred alive in the world.

Chapter 2

And the Word Was Made Man
Challenging the Monopoly of the Word in Christian History

The praxis of Christian feminist theology is most fertile whenever and wherever we are able to hear the symphony of multicultural, multicolored sounds and recognize the voices as at once human, female, and divine.[1]

> There is a true yearning to respond to
> The singing River and the wise Rock.
> So say the Asian, the Hispanic, the Jew
> The African, the Native American, the Sioux,
> The Catholic, the Muslim, the French, the Greek,
> The Irish, the Rabbi, the Priest, the Sheik,
> The Gay, the Straight, the Preacher,
> The privileged, the homeless, the Teacher.
> They hear. They all hear
> The speaking of the Tree
>
> . . . .
> They hear the first and last of every Tree
> Speak to humankind today.
> Come to me,
> Here beside the River.
> Plant yourself beside the River.[2]

Single vision produces worse illusions than double vision or many-headed monsters.[3]

La muerte de mi abuela. Y yo no nunca le hablé en la lengua que entendiera.[4]

I want to hear you. Speak with a woman's tongue. Come out and tell us what time of night it is! Don't let us sink back into silence. If we don't tell our truth, who will?[5]

The above words exemplify the diversity of the voices whose insights and questions can inform the search for more inclusive metaphors of revelation. Some of these voices emerge from an explicitly Christian context while others eschew any particular religious affiliation. Yet given the historical influence of Christianity around the world, rigid and static conceptions of "Word" have served to silence even those voices that have not embraced Christian dogma. Feminist and other theologians, as well as theorists from other disciplines, have begun to raise questions about the authoritarian implications of many expressions of "Word" in Christian thought and practice.

Problematic Conceptions of the Word

Examination of some of the historical developments that have shaped the concept of "Logos" in philosophical thought can reveal the ways in which "Word" came to be identified with ultimate (divine) authority and with elitist and exclusionary language patterns. Contemporary critiques of these developments are important in clarifying the trends within Christianity that have led to a reified and authoritarian "Word." This static conception, as noted earlier, finds its expression in Protestant biblicism and Roman Catholic magisterialism, two distinct but related patterns of claiming authority over the representation of the sacred in the world in ways that silence multiple voices.

The Reification of Logos

Literature in any field relating to religious studies, whether biblical, historical, pastoral, ethical, or theological, abounds with references to "the Word."[6] To understand the significance that concepts of the Word have had in Christian history, however, it is helpful to explore some of the major Greek and Hebrew philosophical meanings of the term.[7] Feminist philosopher Andrea Nye recollects her own feelings of frustration and failure in an early class in logic, where she was told to ignore the meanings of the language in which the problems posed to her were written.[8] Beginning with her own experiences of the separation of words from meaning, Nye goes on to explore the ways in which language has been made increasingly abstract and noncontextual in philosophical logic.

The works of classical philosophers, and especially their logistic systems, have had great influence on white, Western, masculinist philosophical tradition. Nye speaks of Plato as initiating a "logic" that could be broken free from its context and set in a world of "formal differences."[9] He appealed to a preexisting and fixed order of reality and suggested that the task of the philosopher was to discover the "truth" embedded in this reality and to find the language in which to express it so as to make clear its ultimate neutrality.[10]

Given that a single, authoritative truth was held to exist, one that could be defined and defended by the philosopher, the aim of the philosophical project moved beyond persuasion to that of the establishment of a superior and authoritative position, one that could be defended as reflective of a higher reality beyond the realm of material being. Because this "higher reality" was distanced from the realm of materiality, it must be expressed in a language appropriate to its exalted status, that is, a language other than that of everyday communication. Thus both reality and language are reconstituted. These philosophical developments had a great influence on the use of the term "Logos":

> *Logos,* the common Greek word used for all the great variety of kinds of speech, begins to take on the metaphysical weight that will continue to burden it in a long series of philosophical and theological usages. *Logos* no longer can be the simple, ordinary "what someone says," but, as required by logical division, it must be restricted to statements that are either true or false.... Spoken language can be no guide in logical matters, it must be referred to and evaluated in an ideal language that reflects the reality of the Forms.[11]

The connection that Plato established between "Logos" and a highly specialized language form, spoken and understood only by an educated elite, is precursor to the role of Latin within Christianity, an issue to which I return below. And as with the later retention of Latin long after it ceased to be an oral language, the language of Platonic logic effectively silenced the voices of those who did not have privilege of access to intensive formal education. Women, slaves, non-Greek "barbarians," tradespeople, and other workers were not seen as having the capacity to "regulate their feelings and desires in the ways required by logic."[12] The connection between authoritative speech and authoritarian rule was firmly established.

Aristotle moved philosophical logic in a somewhat different direction through the use of the syllogism, which, suggests Nye, made possible not only the articulation of that which was already known but also the control of the production of new knowledge.[13] The mechanisms of the syllogism provided the rules needed to regulate debate, but in light of the possibility for the generation of new knowledge, appeals were not made to a higher authority. Instead, privileged male citizens with access to philosophical education became that authority. Nye suggests that "the ability to reason, to reject the diversity of opinion for Logos, to foresee the conclusions that syllogisms generated, served as a non-bodily mark of those destined to rule."[14] This model of logic based on the syllogism excluded all that was contradictory or considered "irrational," continuing the exclusion of large segments of the population from any voice in academic discourse. Indeed, Aristotle held up an ideal Greek male, which he recognized was not achieved in every Greek man of his time, as the one not only who had exclusive access to the construction and validation of "truth" but upon whom a politics could be developed that used "rationality" as a basis for institutionalizing men's authority over women and slaves.[15]

By the time of Zeno, a Stoic, the Alexandrian empire had opened up a whole new world, and influences and competition from Persia, Africa, and East Asia made it impossible to retain a narrow notion of the Greek citizen as "ideal human being." A broader and more universal concept was required than the Greek male. With the experience of the meetings of diverse human languages, the Stoics engaged in a semantic enterprise in which *meanings* were central, meanings that could be represented in any language. If a logic could be developed that stood above and beyond the limitations of any particular language, a "meta-universe of discourse" would exist and the resulting truth could be posited as universal.[16]

Zeno was also the first major logician to situate his philosophical quest directly in an appeal to divine validation. This shift allowed Zeno and his fellow Stoics to claim that they were not working with mere human inventions, with all the inherent implications of possible fallibility, but were simply following the dictates of God "the divine logician."[17] Truth did not rise and fall with empires but was "objectively" maintained by the supreme being who reveals knowledge to those who represent the best interests of such truth. This truth was now communicated in its own particular expression of language — the language of formal logic.[18] The development of logic did not *begin* the oppression of slaves, women, underclasses, or subject peoples or even play the major role in maintaining such dynamics. But,

> Stoic logic ... provided the grammar for communicative relations
> in a centrally governed world-state, a divinely ordained universal

law that could govern all peoples, and a model for learned discussion that continued to finesse substantive questions of justice and injustice.[19]

This approach to the language of truth, far removed from the vernacular languages spoken by the diverse peoples of a culture, will find parallels in the granting of hegemony to Latin in Roman Catholicism and is a key component in the silencing of a plurality of voices.

The Hebrew tradition had also developed a strong conception of "Word," expressed through the term *dabar*. Particularly important in the prophetic texts of the Hebrew scriptures, *dabar* denotes the Spirit of God speaking through the prophet.[20] A significant difference between Hebrew and Greek thought is that the Hebrew *dabar*, spoken through a prophet by the Spirit of God, is presumably available to all rather than reserved to the educated elite. This is related to "Word" understood more in the sense of everyday communication among people than as embedded in particular expressions of language. The Word referred to in Hebrew thought was primarily the spoken word and thus was "not an inert record but a living something, like sound, something going on."[21] Although the "book, the Law and the Prophets," became more central in Hebrew tradition as Jewish peoples moved through times of conquest and uncertainty, a strong dimension of the multifaceted expressions of "Word" prevented its codification into a rigid authoritarian concept.[22] Jewish tradition has maintained a lively emphasis on the spoken word, although Judaism, as well as Christianity, has succumbed to some extent to a perceived need to define the sacred and to codify both the content that will be passed down as tradition and also the process by which such transmission will occur.

Walter Ong outlines the move from a sense of Word as "a highly auditory sensorium,... a living something, like sound, something going on,"[23] as evidenced in traditional Hebrew understandings, to a feeling that words are most relevant and significant when written or printed.[24] There are two major revolutions in this evolution, alphabetization and the development of movable alphabetic type. In addressing the impact of the first, Ong notes:

> The sense of order and control which the alphabet...imposes is overwhelming. Arrangement in space seemingly provides maximal symbols of order and control, probably because the concepts of order and control are themselves kinesthetically and visually grounded, formed chiefly out of sensory experience involved with space. When the alphabet commits the verbal and conceptual worlds...to the quiescent and obedient order of space, it imputes

to language and to thought an additional consistency of which preliterate persons have no inkling. . . . *It appears no accident that formal logic was invented in an alphabetic culture.*[25]

The developments that came with alphabetization and later with print did not mean a sudden and total disruption of earlier aural and oral modes of communication. Yet the combination of writing and print created the possibility of the solitary, isolated thinker. The scholar with "his" book replaced the interpersonal networks that prevailed as matrices of communication in oral cultures. With the advent of print, "[E]ven words themselves could become property, as the principle of copyright came into being and was finally taken for granted."[26]

When words became property, so did ideas. And knowledge that could be not only preserved but also created and possessed by a solitary thinker, further and further removed from the people whose lives would be affected by his ponderings and pronouncements, was typified and entrenched by the use of Latin for all scholarly discourse. This language was "a symbol of the old oral-aural world where the orator was the perfectly educated man," despite the fact that, by the sixteenth century, Latin had been completely stripped of any roots in oral-aural culture for an entire millennium.[27] The whole existence of Latin, from the time of classical antiquity, has depended on script, and the language has not, since that time, been spoken by anyone who could not write it. But Latin is no mere "dead" language. To the contrary, it was — and is — used continually for the invention of new words and for new meanings for old words.[28] This language, which has for centuries been limited to print in terms of its usage, continues to exert immense influence on the linguistic development of English and the romance languages that emerged from Latin roots.

The use of Latin exemplifies the split between oral and written language. The impact of this split is related to the development of dictionaries in the eighteenth century. Suggesting that dictionaries are created for the purpose of establishing "total written control over the written word," Ong states that these mechanisms can give the spoken language of a people an inflexibility similar to that of Learned Latin.[29]

The emphasis in Ong's work is on highlighting the ways in which glimpses of the significance of oral-aural communication have been kept alive throughout history, particularly Christian history, a project related to my own current attempt to recover silenced voices. Ong does *not*, however, adequately address the extremes to which the developments he outlines have affected the Christian enterprise in terms of its potential toward authoritarianism.[30]

Logos and Authority

Two contemporary manifestations of Christian hegemony of the Word, Protestant biblicism and Catholic magisterialism, are rooted in historical understandings of the Word of God as they have developed throughout Western Christian theological thought. Although I shall discuss the distinctiveness of each expression below, I am concerned here with the ways in which both reside in similar interpretations of the authority of the Word. Both appeal to particular understandings of revelation, and both exclude the experiences and participation of large numbers of Christian peoples.

Dorothee Sölle notes an emphasis on obedience as the key virtue by which the good Christian could be known and insists that in terms of the focus on acquiescence, there is no notable distinction between Protestant and Catholic positions.[31] Whether obedience is due to a particular understanding of scriptural authority or to the teaching authority of the magisterium, the outcome is similar. In particular, insists Sölle, the emphasis on submissive compliance, whether to Bible or church, ignores the fact that "in Jesus' proclamation the world takes on a concrete reality to be reckoned with," a reality that must be continually reshaped in the light of emerging demands for justice. Instead, the focus on obedience leads to identification of the world with a given order.[32] Similar parallels might be observed in an exploration of "fundamentalist" approaches to religious belief.[33]

Understandings of authority that are promoted by religious structures and institutions are central both in determining and in expressing these institutions' approaches to divine revelation. What does it mean to grant ultimate authority to scripture or church? How have interpretations and expressions of authority changed over the years? And where does personal and communal self-determination and accountability interact with authoritarian structures, whether written, spoken, or implied?

The etymology of the word "authority" reveals that its root, *augere,* means "to make to grow or increase." In her provocative book on authority, feminist theorist Kathleen Jones challenges all conceptions of authority as sovereignty.[34] She discusses sovereign authority in terms similar to those used to justify Logos (above), positing that "political authority is defined as the rightful imposition of order on disorder."[35] This question of *rightful* imposition is of critical importance. When the basic assumption behind understandings of authority is that some do indeed have the right to command, and all others have the duty to obey, even extensive participation by diverse persons in political and other institutions "merely increases the number of those whose consent is required and whose obligations are expected to be fulfilled."[36]

The authority of the Logos of the philosophers, and later of Christian teaching, has influenced greatly both ecclesial and political structures. During the sixteenth century, this tradition was developed in the more explicitly theological terms of the divine right of kings:

> The imperative mood of kingly dictates came to rest on the same foundation as the necessity to submit to the will of God. Divine right theories supported the right of kings to rule through their claims to patrilineal descent from Adam, the original earthly sovereign. These theories contended that dominion had been granted by God to Adam and had passed, through patrilineal descent, to subsequent generations of kings whose claim to rule was based on their established heritage. . . . Paternal and regal authority, domestic and political rule, were completely identified.[37]

A quest for political and ecclesial systems that are just and participative mandates the development and implementation of alternative understandings of authority that will truly "augment and enable to grow." When authority is understood in growth-producing ways, it is neither coercive nor dictatorial. While this interpretation is rare in Christian tradition, it is not absent. Delores Williams, in examining the use of biblical stories within African-American communities, notes how slave men and women

> created an oral text from a written text. . . . They composed this oral text by extracting from the Bible or adding to biblical content those phrases, stories, biblical personalities and moral prescriptions relevant to the character of their life-situation and pertinent to the aspirations of the slave community. They took from the Bible those things that assured them that they were under God's care, that God would eventually bring justice to their cause.[38]

Claudia Camp insists that "to say that scripture has true authority over us . . . is to imply that we have . . . *freely* placed our decision-making processes into its hands."[39] Camp insists that no loss of freedom or agency is involved in placing oneself in relationship with this authority, although her use of the word "over" in referring to this relationship suggests that she still understands authority as "benign" sovereignty.

No less with scripture than with any other "authority," relationship is central, a relationship that authentically seeks the growth and empowerment of the self and the other. Tom Driver, insisting that "neither scripture nor tradition has any authority by itself," suggests that biblical scholarship would be well served by academicians entering into a relationship with people in local churches. In such a way, scholars might rediscover their capacity to ask the questions that are important to the people in the pews, and the people might rediscover their own authority in shaping the expression and interpretation of their faith.[40] A psychologically mature church would "ask of scripture, 'who gave you the authority to be our text of reference?' And it should answer: 'We did.' "[41] In such a relationship, the rigid "Word" yields to a mutual dialogue that includes both scripture and tradition *and* diverse human voices. Authority is freely granted to those sources that have come to be trusted in their capacity to enhance the growth and life in the world of the community. As in any mutual dialogue, *both* parties are changed in the process — and canonical texts are no exception. Such an understanding is not reflected in relationships of authoritarianism, whether that control is exerted by the written text of scripture or by the Vatican magisterium.

The Word of the Bible

The long process of the recording, "reproduction," and "dissemination" of the canonical text that we recognize as the Bible parallels developments in alphabetization and print. The storytelling cultures out of which the biblical narratives emerged passed on their tales in terms of themes and actions: verbatim repetition was neither a possibility nor a value.[42] Even the medieval scholastics did not read the scriptures much, by comparison with post-typographical theologians. Rather, they *recited* them, as the Greeks recited Homer.[43] A canon shared in this way was not confined to the static, literalist interpretation that is characteristic of contemporary biblicism. The *codification* of the canon in written form changed the former fluidity of interpretation and had far-reaching implications for conceptions of revelation. If a particular written document could be said to contain a full and sufficient revelation of God's Word to "his" people, ongoing direct revelation need no longer be considered available to the people as a whole. And this codified recording of God's Word, entrusted into the safe-keeping of powerful religious leaders, could no longer be easily revised when circumstances changed.[44]

From a historical viewpoint, it is not surprising that the Protestant Reformation, with its increased emphasis on *sola scriptura* as the source of salvation, occurred within the century following the invention of the printing press. As scandals and outrages abounded within the hierarchical structures of the institutional church, Martin Luther and his followers had found in the now readily available texts resources to challenge the abuses they encountered. No longer were the faithful dependent upon "the Word" as it was interpreted and filtered down to them from church authorities, in a language they neither spoke nor understood. Yet the stage was also set for a rigidity regarding the relationship of text and "Word" that Luther and his colleagues could not have foreseen.

An important distinction must be made between an appreciation of biblical texts as authoritative in the sense of empowering and conducive to growth and the biblicism under discussion here. In an "ascending" view, the focus is on the community of believers that "accepts the writings of certain individuals as sacred to them and eventually comes to regard them as the word of God." The faith and experience of the *community* is what determines the validity and privileged place given to particular writings. By contrast, in the "descending" view, "[T]he word of God comes to a human author who gives it form and expression, and the believers accept it for what it is, the infallible word of God."[45]

From the perspective of twentieth-century believers from diverse cultures and languages, divine inspiration in the descending view must be extended beyond that originally visited upon the prophet or apostle to "textual critics and copyists, to translators and interpreters."[46] Those most determined to subscribe to the "descending" approach to divine inspiration often do not recognize the interpreted nature of any translation. Ironically, many of those who most adamantly defend scripture as the literal Word of God rely on such paraphrased versions as *The Living Word,* editions that are mediated still further than are more literal translations.

A withdrawal into literalism in the search for certainty and dependable answers is a relatively common reaction in today's world when change and *un*certainty are the normative experience. When everything seems unstable and "relative," the idea of an inerrant and divinely inspired Bible provides a stable foundation upon which one may count absolutely. Sally McFague links this search for certainty with contemporary fears of pluralism and particularly with the "fear of relativizing Scripture through historical criticism":

> The Bible is a sacred text, different from all other texts, and not relative and pluralistic as are all other human products. The Bible becomes an idol: the fallible, human words of Scripture are understood as referring correctly and literally to God. Even where these sentiments are not expressed clearly or in such extreme fashion, religious literalism remains a powerful current in our society.[47]

Even liberal theologies tend to either literalize or spiritualize the symbols used to express sacred reality, thus freezing these symbols in time and space rather than allowing them the dynamism of growth and movement that is characteristic of life and vitality.

Disputing the rigid and authoritarian nature of much biblicism is not to deny the need all peoples have for their sacred texts. A body of knowledge, accessible across multiple generations and linking communities around the world, provides a continuous sense of tradition that, at its best, empowers and engenders a profound sense of historical and contemporary connection. Delores Williams insists that "a slave cultural heritage,...patterned by biblical motifs, is the context of the early Christian origins of African Americans" and is thus of crucial importance to contemporary womanist scholars.[48] Elisabeth Schüssler Fiorenza also makes a case for the importance of historical memory:

> Liberation movements have pointed out that it is a sign of oppression not to have a written history and historical self-identity. History is not a collection of facts or a meaningless chronicle, but either a means of domination or the heritage of a people that looks to the past for its vision of the future. Therefore, if oppressed peoples are to have a future, freedom, and autonomy, they must recover their historical roots and base their solidarity on a common historical self-understanding.[49]

If the recovery of historical roots is vital to Schüssler Fiorenza's own biblical theological enterprise, so too is the need to reject "textual absolutism" and to trace and appreciate the relationships and interactions between any texts and the socio-political realities from which they emerge and into which they are inserted.[50] Through the *rhetoric* of interpretation that Schüssler Fiorenza proposes, movement is made possible into a dialogic relationship with biblical texts that challenges not only interpretation but the texts themselves, inviting a shift in focus from "the androcentric linguistic medium" to the act of reading. When language is seen as a structure affected and transformed by social conditions, "then writing, translation, and interpretation become acts of struggle for change."[51] In this paradigm, the canon is no longer a set of definitive norms but rather offers models "of struggles and visions that are open to their own transformations through the power of the Spirit in ever new sociohistorical locations."[52]

A biblicist approach to canonical scripture cannot account for the ways in which historical institutional Christianity has excluded and actively oppressed whole communities of peoples or for the ways in which many such communities have indeed reinterpreted the biblical stories in the service of the survival of their people.[53] The rhetorical interpretive model theorized by Schüssler Fiorenza, which insists that such communities "interrogate biblical texts for religious visions that foster equality, justice, and the logic of the *ekklesia* rather than that of patriarchal domination," relocates "authority" in the potential for liberation and provides the possibility of sustaining life-enhancing connections to biblical sources.[54]

Roman Catholic Monopoly of "the Word" Metaphor: The Word of the Church

In a 1925 publication, Spanish statesman, orator, and publicist Juan Donoso Cortés attacks the liberalism and socialism of his day with a vehement defense of the Catholic Church:

> The Catholic Church, as a religious institution, has exercised the same influence in society that Catholicism, as a doctrine, has exercised in the world; the same that our Lord Jesus Christ has exercised in man. And the reason is this: that our Lord Jesus Christ, His doctrine and His Church, are in reality only three different manifestations of the same thing — that is, the divine action supernaturally and simultaneously working in man and in all his faculties, in society and in all its institutions. Our Lord Jesus Christ, Catholicism, and the Catholic Church are the same word — the word of God perpetually resounding from the heavens.[55]

Although mainstream Roman Catholic thought even in Donoso Cortés's day was not quite so brash as to claim such identification between Jesus and the Catholic Church, this statement is only an exaggeration of a mind-set that I will call "magisterialist." In the case just cited the church is set against the state, but the alliance of church and state since the conversion of Constantine lies behind much of the power dynamic that continues to influence institutional — that is, *Roman* — Catholicism. Rosemary Radford Ruether observes that "the pope himself continues to combine these two roles as bishop of Rome and religious head of the Catholic Church and also political head of the Vatican state as an internationally recognized political entity."[56]

In the first four centuries of Christianity, dramatic departures were made from the revolutionary conceptions of authority that many see embodied in Jesus. Jesus' practice of authority transformed the notion of accountability, particularly in reference to Christian leaders. These individuals were to consider themselves accountable both to God and to their communities, in a model of servanthood. Yet by the fifth century,

Pope Leo I would claim a degree and style of sovereignty reminiscent of the Roman imperial dictatorship. The claim to a "divine right" to lord it over everyone else had the effect of eliminating the particular accountability of leaders.[57] Despite periodic attempts to challenge an increasingly authoritarian church, the development of a centralized and autocratic "monarchy," particularly after the Gregorian Reform of the eleventh century, was a major factor contributing to the sixteenth-century Reformation.[58] And if such an approach *led* to the Protestant Reformation, it was only reinforced in its aftermath. Although much of this rigidity would not be codified until the reign of Pius IX in the nineteenth century, when Vatican I met, these earlier influences, based in Thomist theology and philosophy and thus free of any "taint of modern influence," became ossified as the normative Catholic intellectual system.[59]

The conception of authority operative in these developments is parallel to that operating in the extreme biblicism described above. As Monika Hellwig points out, this understanding "assumes that revelation is not a continuing reality in the lives of all who are open to God's presence and call, but rather a finite reality that has been captured and codified and entrusted to certain office-holders to be taught and applied to others."[60] Vatican actions (for example, the "disciplining" of the signers of a *New York Times* advertisement claiming a plurality of Catholic opinions on abortion and the dismissal of Charles Curran from Catholic University in Washington, D.C.) indicate that Vatican II discussions about collegiality remain on the level of rhetoric and have little reality in practice. Significant theological discourse about the issues involved is rejected in favor of authoritarian demands for obedience. It is "the scandal of dissent itself" that is challenged rather than the truth of the positions taken.[61] Instead of a closed canon of scripture that allows for no new interpretation, Catholic magisterialism upholds a closed canon of law and order, encased still in the trappings of the absolute monarchies of the late Roman and Byzantine empires. Edmund Hill writes:

> [The pope] officially resides in a "Sacred Palace"; his court is divided into "Sacred Congregations"; he is assisted by the "Sacred College of Cardinals"; he is the "most holy Lord," "the Holy Father"; he was until recently crowned with a triple tiara.... Only in the present pontificate...have some of these trappings, *but none of the substance,* of absolute monarchy been laid aside.[62]

Despite the more collegial language that emerged from Vatican II, and the hope that it engendered, contemporary experiences of a monarchical system dictating "the Word" to a less and less "listening" church point to the accuracy of Hill's observation that "none of the substance" has changed. Indeed, rhetoric about the church as "the people of God" has encouraged large numbers of Catholics to so identify themselves, in parish or base community groups, and to attribute a diminishing sense of credibility to "the other church," the one in Rome that is experienced as at best irrelevant.[63]

The Triumph of the Word

Women, and others whose voices have been excluded from the "authoritative" structures of white, Western, masculinist theological thought, have never been entirely silenced, yet the cost has been, and is, great. In a moving analysis of Anne Sexton's poem "The Jesus Papers," Alicia Ostriker notes the extent to which the poet has herself internalized the Christian message of sacrifice and has identified the authoritarian church pronouncements with God. "However relentless her critique of male authority, she sees no way out of it," says Ostriker. "She has had many words, but God, who is Logos, has the last word."[64] From the perspective of literary criticism, Ostriker observes the devastating consequences of the metaphoric monopoly of a static Word that freezes revelation at a particular point in time and within a specific text or context. A similar criticism may be offered from the perspective of Christian theology. Change was central in many of Jesus' teachings, and the possibility of transformation and conversion was ever-present. Yet "the same Jesus who had taught that nothing is final except the kingdom of God in the present-future, was proclaimed to have been the final form of God. He became not only 'the Word of God' but God's *last* word."[65]

Protestant biblicism and Catholic magisterialism, in their identification respectively of scripture and the church with the "Word of God," either explicitly or in practice, promote disempowerment. Persons are no longer encouraged to see the possibility of or to take responsibility for participating in the ongoing life of the sacred in the world. Humans are immersed in their own personal worlds, frequently isolated from one another and the natural universe, spectators and manipulators rather than participants. This image is vastly different from the one suggested by Nelle Morton as she reflects on the ways in which she has experienced women coming to new awarenesses of sacred power in their lives:

> Every liberation movement rises out of its bondage with a new speech on its lips.... To evoke her story to speech woman experiences an imperative — a prior great Listening Ear,... an ear which hears her without interruption down through her defenses, clichéd

language, pretensions, evasions, pervasive hurts, angers, frustra-
tions, internalized stereotyped images until she experiences at the
lowest point of her life that she is sustained.[66]

With this perception of Morton's in mind, I turn to some contemporary feminist theological attempts to reimage the metaphors that have
dominated Christian tradition.

The White Christian-Feminist Search
for Alternative Metaphors

White Christian-feminist theologians have engaged the metaphors of
their tradition in multiple ways. Some of these efforts have particular
potential to assist in challenging the dominance of the Word metaphor in
such a way as to bring into theo-ethical discourse the voices that express
multiple, previously excluded experiences.[67] Throughout this section, I
use the work of *white* feminist theologians because I share closely their
accountability for the transformation of racist systems of exclusion,
including theo-ethical systems, which is the task of the works under
discussion. The insights that these projects provide offer suggestions
and provocative possibilities for further exploration of alternative theo-
ethical metaphors. Because of the ways in which the image of Wisdom
once coexisted with Word, I begin my exploration with a consideration
of feminist appropriations of Sophia/Wisdom.

Sophia

Logos and Sophia have fulfilled similar functions in providing founda-
tional explanatory conceptions for the organizational principles behind
the cosmos and the relationship between God and humans. But the identification of Logos with the male Jesus in early Christianity led to the
subsequent obscuring of the female personification of Sophia.[68]

There are two significant dimensions that Wisdom tradition emphasized in the context of Hebrew culture. First, there was a major emphasis
on the lessons and significance of human experience and the capacity to
examine critically this experience and make decisions based on this examination. Second, the relationship between creator and creation was
seen to be central. Susan Cady, Marian Ronan, and Hal Taussig suggest
that a shift in Hebrew theology, from a focus on the history of Israel to
concern about the creation of the world, distances God somewhat from
"his" creation and thus allows an Israel that has been "dominated, con-
quered, divided, exiled, and imperialized" to maintain faith in a God

who is now removed from such developments.[69] Yet this determination to maintain relationship with God in the face of oppressive social and political reality, reflected in the face of Sophia, was a continuing source of empowerment in the ongoing survival struggles of the Jewish people.

The characteristics of Sophia/Wisdom, as they are exemplified in the literature of the Hebrew scriptures, suggest a divine power that is nurturing yet strong and full of compassion and commitment to her people. Elisabeth Schüssler Fiorenza summarizes these characteristics:

> Divine Wisdom speaks with pride among her people. She offers life, rest, knowledge, and the abundance of creation to all who accept her. She is all-powerful, intelligent, unique, people-loving, an initiate of God's knowledge, a collaborator in God's work. She is the leader on the way out of the bondage of Egypt, the preacher and teacher in Israel, and the architect of God's creation. She shares the throne of God and lives in symbiosis with the Divine. One can sense how much the language of the biblical texts speaks of her struggles to characterize Chokma-Sophia as divine in the theological framework of monotheism.[70]

Little specific teaching content is present in the Wisdom passages, and few moral exhortations. Rather, the emphasis is on Sophia's relationship with the listener and with divine reality, and she becomes "both teacher and that which is taught."[71] This same trend is evident in relation to Jesus in the Gospel of John where "Jesus as teacher borders on arrogance and contentlessness."[72] Yet Sophia flies in the face of prevailing emphases on an increasingly abstract Logos by encouraging — even demanding — continuing reflection on and participation in the life of the world. In addition, and perhaps most significantly, Sophia brings her gender, "no small matter in a tradition which defined itself by its monotheism in contrast to the worship of gods and goddesses in the surrounding cultures."[73] These characteristics of Sophia are inherent in the understanding of the sacred demonstrated by Jesus and his immediate followers:

> The earliest Jesus traditions perceive this God of gracious goodness in a woman's *Gestalt* and divine *Sophia* (wisdom). The very old saying "Sophia is justified [or vindicated] by all her children" (Luke 7:35[Q]) probably had its setting in Jesus' table community with tax collectors, prostitutes, and sinners, as well.[74]

In observing that the Sophia figure in the Wisdom literature is frequently one who is spurned and not "successful" in the way in which the awaited Messiah is depicted, Cady, Ronan, and Taussig make a compelling case for a Jesus who is perceived more as a Wisdom figure than the awaited Messiah.[75] In addition, Sophia is bearer of creative power, strong and assertive to the point of prophetic anger, yet retaining an image of warmth and nurturance.[76] Gospel descriptions of Jesus differ from this account only in his maleness.

One can only hypothesize the extent to which the personification of Wisdom as female, and the perceived danger of such personification as a threat to monotheism, are responsible for the overwhelming of Sophia by the male Logos. The sense of a Sophia who "shares the throne of God" will ultimately become abhorrent to both Jewish and Christian proponents of a rigid monotheism. Occasional glimpses of a more inclusive tradition continue to offer alternative interpretations of divine presence,[77] but the Logos/Word will dominate theological thought and discourse through the twentieth century. To what extent might a metaphor of voices, and the development of a methodology with which to embody this metaphor in theo-ethical discourse, take up again the potential inherent in Sophia/Wisdom and move forward the task of creating a more just and inclusive life for earth and all its inhabitants?

Sharon Welch: *A Feminist Ethic of Risk*

Sharon Welch's *A Feminist Ethic of Risk* is important because she includes voices from black women's literature as sources for developing her "ethic of risk."[78] It is helpful to examine Welch's project as she defines it, before applying the criteria developed above to assess the extent to which her text promotes the empowerment of multiple voices in theo-ethical discourse.

Welch begins with an analysis of the ways in which the contemporary nuclear world reflects an "ethic of control," one that is responsible both for the oppression and exploitation of millions of earth's people and the earth itself and also for the "culture of despair" that pervades people of goodwill who would be about the work of social transformation. This culture of despair arises out of our internalization of the ethic of control, in that we are devastated when we cannot control the outcome of our resistance actions and see immediate results. To combat the resulting loss of hope, Welch posits an "ethic of risk" and suggests that materials from communities that have survived through vicious exploitation and oppression can provide a moral resource for white, middle-class activists to overcome their tendency to paralyzing despair.

Welch's description of the development and pervasiveness of the "culture of control and despair" is compelling. The link she makes between, on one hand, military ideals of total security, invulnerability, and response to force with force, and, on the other hand, the Euro-American, middle-class belief that "to be responsible means that one can ensure that the aim of one's action will be carried out," is important and insightful.[79] This drive for certainty and security is reflected in the swing to fundamentalist religion — both biblicist and magisterialist — and politics. By contrast, Welch suggests placing our efforts for transformation in a communal context that empowers us in the present by enabling us to see our efforts as part of a greater struggle stretching into both past and future. Bringing our voices into dialogue, for the purpose of mutual critique, means taking one another seriously as moral agents across the lines of differences that divide us. This requires an understanding of community that is not immersed in individual identity but that insists that we "cannot be moral alone" as individuals or as homogeneous groups.[80] To what extent is Welch's book helpful in promoting authentic discourse among diverse peoples?

Different, Not "Other": In advocating an approach that acknowledges differences yet eschews encountering those embodying these differences as totally "other," care must be taken not to err in the direction of once again moving too quickly to seek similarities or common ground. Welch comes close to collapsing significant differences in the use she makes of her resources:

> From those courageously facing and struggling against an oppression they have not yet fully overcome, we can learn how we, too, can join the struggle against racism and persist in our work against other structural problems, problems that have as little chance of being easily overcome as does racism.[81]

Regardless of her frequent references to the need to bear power differentials in mind, Welch's minimization of the differences between racism and "other structural problems" can lead to co-optation or at best a failure to acknowledge that *our* relationship to the undoing of racism is vastly different from that of African-American people. The other issues where we might use the insights gained, while having certain similarities, will need their own analysis and strategies for sustaining struggle in the long term. There is insufficient attention throughout the text to the cause and effect relationship of the privilege Welch mentions and the oppression described in the texts she uses, a shortcoming that might be attributed to Welch's reluctance to impute evil or bad intent to anyone. This is not to say that the insights to which Welch refers *cannot* be helpful to others, as they clearly have been to her. The other extreme is seeing those in dominated communities as nothing more than victims, a trap that Welch successfully avoids. This is an ongoing issue in feminist/womanist/mujerista efforts to use one another's work with integrity.

Passionate Commitment: Welch's text is engaged and often moving. Much of Welch's content is designed to move people of goodwill beyond what she calls "middle-class numbness and cynicism" into sustained engagement with the world around them, engagement that will include joy and celebration as well as grief and pain.[82] Risking action, rather than retreating into numbness and death, can be a source of passionate joy. Welch's insistence on the integrally connected nature of passionate anger, love, and celebration is a major strength of *A Feminist Ethic of Risk*. Yet when Welch speaks of the need to know "refugees and the poor" in order to "sustain rage, because one [becomes] aware of the value of the lives being so unnecessarily damaged or destroyed,"[83] she does not pay adequate attention to the potentially tokenizing implications of such a statement. What does it mean to "*know* refugees and the poor"? Given Welch's insistence on such knowledge, either from texts such as those she uses as resources or from concrete physical interaction, her own text is curiously lacking as to where her own "passionate commitment" lies in terms of her continuing growth into "reciprocity" in her appropriation of the works of African-American women.

Responsibility and Relationship: Questions of responsibility and accountability are difficult to discern in Welch's text, largely because she minimizes the reality of evil intent in her quest for empowerment of herself and her community of peace activists. While many oppressive and destructive systems take on a certain life of their own, resulting in consequences that no one foresaw, let alone intended, Welch overstates the case when she asserts that "well-intentioned people are responsible for the arms race."[84] And the intentional misinformation fed to the American public during the Gulf War of January 1992 to prevent our knowledge of the extent of Iraqi civilian and other casualties was *not* the decision of well-intentioned people. On the other hand, Welch does ground her work in her own community of middle-class peace activists and accepts responsibility for her social location: "We ... are not responsible for others; we are responsible for ourselves — for seeing the limits of our own vision and for rectifying the damages caused by the arrogant violation of those limits."[85]

Welch's claim that the women's movement has become, "only through long struggle, a movement more inclusive of the pain and wisdom of women of all races and classes" is indicative of at best a certain naiveté, if not ignorance, in terms of the distance that is yet to be traveled.[86] In light of such statements, I must wonder whether the texts of African-American women have been adequately utilized by Welch to further her own consciousness of the extent to which power differentials still exist, particularly within feminist movements. I do not suggest that texts from diverse contexts have no insights to offer other than in regard to our own relationship to them through structures of power and domination. But those in a position of social power in relationship to any text must take, as a primary challenge, the responsibility for learning that which is most central to the authors of the texts. References to the lived experience of racism are peripheral in Welch's text to the major task of developing an alternative ethic based on risk and communication rather than control. A focus on the moral wisdom to be learned from African-American women, when not accompanied by a clear understanding of the unequal power relationships that still exist between black and white women in twentieth-century U.S. society, runs the risk of appropriation without reciprocity.[87]

Beyond Identity to Praxis: In moving to a focus on praxis, the issue of identity is not to be eliminated but rather is seen as a strategy for moving to empowerment and action. While Welch does not delineate her project in terms of a heavy emphasis on identity, neither does she develop her ethic in such a way that her readers gain a sense of where to move in order to engage in liberative praxis. Although insisting that conversation is not enough and positing working together as that which "enables genuine conversation to occur,"[88] Welch never tells us how we "get from here to there." Rather, she merely claims that it can be done:

> Middle-class people can be challenged by the fragile power of love and justice to move from cultured despair to learned hope. With this shift, critique can serve as a foundation for more nuanced strategies of resistance and a catalyst for further work.... Without working with others on projects geared toward social change, it is impossible to maintain the vision and energy necessary to sustain long-term work.[89]

Just how those who are mired in despair are to dredge up the will and energy to engage in this work that Welch deems essential is not addressed. The novels Welch discusses in *A Feminist Ethic of Risk* indicate the extent to which ideals and practical action are held as integral to one another by those whose lives are profoundly affected by exploitation and domination. We must hold a healthy skepticism as to the capacity of words about love, joy, hope, and connectedness, which Welch develops in her final chapter, to hold those of us who wield privilege in racist society accountable for our role in sustaining domination and exploitation. While we must indeed frequently risk taking action with no guarantee that the desired outcome will be achieved, such action must be rooted both in a utopic sense of an idealized world to be hoped for in the future *and* in a realistic appraisal of the forces with which we must contend today. The failure to posit some suggestions about how to begin to move from our current point of despair to one of creative, engaged action is ironic in a volume that purports to be an "ethic," and particularly one of risk.

Transformation of Theological Method: A major strength in Welch's text is in her revisioning of theological content, where she suggests the danger of conceptions of divine omnipotence for white, middle-class people. This concept assumes that "absolute power can be a good."[90] Welch details the ways in which this image of omnipotence, in the context of exploitative and dominating cultures, has served to perpetuate domination when it has been embraced by those in power. Privileged men in power in church and society are enabled by theories of divine omnipotence to "represent" such a God. To counter this oppressing image, Welch insists that the divine not only is *in* but *is* relational power.[91] The Nazi Holocaust and "the many genocides of Western history" suggest the *fragility* of holy power.[92] The emphasis on human agency suggested by Welch's alternative conception is important for any theology that has the potential to transform more than our personal perceptions.

If a major strength of Welch's text lies in its theological content, the chief weakness is in her methodology. Welch's use of African-American novelists and other theorists is restricted almost entirely to the four chapters in which the novels form the experiential basis of her work. Apart from an occasional name or notation, African-American voices are noticeably lacking from the remainder of the text where Welch critiques past theory and sets up her own constructive project. This lends credence to the possibility that, once again, voices from another culture have been used to provide the narrative required to ground the work, but they apparently do not have anything to do with the creation of theory. bell hooks describes the problems thus created:

> In many feminist theory classes, this problem is addressed by including work that is taken to represent "real life" experience or fictional portrayals of concrete reality along with work that is deemed highly theoretical. Often such attempts reinforce racism

and elitism by identifying writing by working-class women and women of color as "experiential" while the writing of white women represents "theory."[93]

I do not suggest that the texts used by Welch — novels written by African-American women — cannot be used in the creation of theory. On the contrary, this is part of the methodological transformation called for. What is significant here is that Welch does *not* so use these texts in any observable way. Patricia Hill Collins, who herself uses much narrative from the lives of working-class African-American women, suggests that such an enterprise is central to "reclaiming the Black feminist intellectual tradition":

> Reclaiming the Black feminist intellectual tradition involves...
> challenging the very definitions of intellectual discourse.... Re-
> claiming the Black women's intellectual tradition involves exam-
> ining the everyday ideas of Black women not previously consid-
> ered intellectuals.... Musicians, vocalists, poets, writers, and other
> artists constitute another group of Black women intellectuals who
> have aimed to interpret Black women's experiences.[94]

Together, hooks and Collins offer a challenge that must be addressed by all who would attempt to authentically integrate more diverse voices into their work.

The use of intercultural resources can never be considered "recipro-cal" if the method and goals of the reader are not radically transformed in the process. By limiting the works of African-American women, from which she claims to gain her insight, to the initial section of her work, Welch limits the effectiveness of her text. It is an inexplicable con-tradiction on the one hand to refute epistemologies and systems of "knowledge" that continue to exert power over dominated groups and on the other hand to continue to privilege the theories of dominating ideologies and use them to validate insights gained from dominated groups. When white feminist scholars refuse to resort to such valida-tion and allow the alternative visions present in a multiplicity of voices to shape not only the content but also the structure and theoretical im-plications of their work, the conversations suggested by Welch will be closer to becoming a reality.

Susan Thistlethwaite: *Sex, Race, and God*

The critical challenge of the book *Sex, Race, and God* lies in the author's insistence that an exclusivist approach to feminist theology, one that does not adequately engage in conversation among diverse women, cannot be transformed without white women recognizing the long history of distorted racial relationships that still affect their efforts at dialogue.[95] As Susan Thistlethwaite points out, the institution of slavery and the racist structures that have been maintained in the years since emancipation mean that black and white women experience differently most dimensions of their lives. The appeal to experience that has been central in feminist theological work, however, has been for the most part the experience of privileged white women and has silenced the voices of other women in ways similar to the hegemony exercised historically by white male scholars. Critical interrogation is required of anything that is named as "women's experience."[96] Thistlethwaite explores some of the differences between diverse women's experiences through attention to basic Christian concerns about creation, sin, Jesus, and names for God. She then posits violence as a "difference in common" among women. How do the criteria suggested above inform an assessment of the capacity of Thistlethwaite's work to empower dialogue across lines of difference?

Relationship and Otherness: Because the areas of relationship and otherness coinhere so closely in my analysis of *Sex, Race, and God,* I avoid repetitiveness by treating them together. The major strengths and limitations of this text lie in the tensions between relationship and otherness. For example, while Thistlethwaite takes very seriously the relationship of white women to institutional racism, particularly as it was experienced during slavery, she insists that a responsible posture for her to assume in her own personal relationship to black women is one of "otherness."[97] Her insistence on the need for contemporary white feminists to incorporate the awareness of difference into their work, and to acknowledge the ways in which they and their foresisters have been and are "related" to racist practices, is a necessary corrective to the domination of much feminist discourse by white women. Yet a focus on "otherness" can obscure the fact that it is the very fractured and oppressive *relationships* between and among diverse persons and groups that cause exploitation, suffering, and the paralyzing fragmentation that is antithetical to engaged dialogue and political action.

Thistlethwaite rightly emphasizes the dangers of appeals to unity and oneness. For example, many white women have developed theories that view creation as originally pristine and harmonious and themselves as intrinsically related to this natural harmony in some way. Such a view ignores the socio-historical construction of both culture *and* what we view as nature, as well as bypassing the experiences of diverse peoples. Yet to challenge this trend by positing as necessary a politically disastrous polarization between human and other creation, and black and white women, cannot ultimately further the cause of authentic liberation for oppressed peoples or for the earth itself. Regardless of the distorted relationships that exist within the world, we need an increasing rather than decreasing consciousness of the ways in which actions and events in any part of that world ultimately affect all others. This need not imply some original harmony and must certainly include particular emphasis on the relationships of oppression and exploitation that exist. Beverly Harrison, for example, does not advocate easy and uncritical relationship, but she does insist that

> [t]o speak of a theology of relation...is, above all, to insist on the deep, total sociality of all things....Nothing living is self-contained; if there were such a thing as an unrelated individual, none of us would know it.... Our life is part of a vast cosmic web, and no moral theology that fails to envisage reality in this way will be able to make sense of our lives or actions today.[98]

And while acknowledging that "the slow genocide of poor black women, children and men" must remain foremost in the womanist theologian's commitment, Delores Williams insists that such women must "advocate and participate in dialogue and action with *many* diverse social, political, and religious communities concerned about human survival and a productive quality of life for the oppressed."[99] An exaggerated focus on "difference" as something that makes us totally other to one another can result in white feminists once again focusing on their own agenda, however noble it may appear, thus avoiding the very real struggles to which they might contribute by following the lead of women already so engaged.

Regardless of the validity of Thistlethwaite's claim that premature bonding "belongs to the temptations of white women and not only to their graces,"[100] we cannot afford to give up the goal of a renewed expression of relationship across the many differences that currently are systemically organized into oppressive institutional realities. The critical work of justice-making will not wait for women in their multi-identities to work through their own individual issues before engaging in coalition work. Given the tendency of white women to withdraw from situations in which they are challenged or made to feel uncomfortable, an insistence on retaining the possibility of connection in the midst of differences seems more ethically and politically committed than does an insistence on "difference" per se.

Passion: The passion of justifiable anger that gives rise to commitments to justice is evident throughout Thistlethwaite's text. She claims anger as a vital resource for white feminists as they address the ways in which they, too, have been diminished even by the racist system from which they have "benefited."[101] The historical material and the persuasive argument offered of the ways in which white and black women have been set against each other have the capacity to engage readers through the righteous anger that fuels the text itself.

On the other hand, there does not appear to be room in Thistlethwaite's agenda for times of celebration and joy that are essential to maintaining energy for the long-term tasks of liberation. In addition to the *failures* of white feminists both today and in the past, there is a certain history of resistance that must not be lost in self-accusation and guilt. Thistlethwaite is careful to articulate the dangers of paralyzing guilt, yet it is not clear just how such guilt is to be avoided without a multifaceted approach that leaves room for rejoicing in small victories. In addition to analyzing current problems and limitations, all theo-ethicists of liberation need to create space for the renewal of energies in dreaming and envisioning new possibilities. The articulation of images of a future in which differences are freed from the social structures that define them in terms of injustice becomes a creative source of empowerment.

From Identity to Praxis: The lack of a clear-cut sense of a community of accountability and support may be the single most disempowering effect of years of liberal individualism and has led to many contemporary white feminist efforts to establish a sense of "home." Yet Thistlethwaite is right to note that "what is often labeled sisterhood is in fact sometimes economic and ethnic solidarity" and that this bonding has a different and potentially oppressive face when it takes place among those who have privileged access to the sources of institutional and other societal power.[102] Unfortunately, she does not identify the distinctions that exist among women within the racial categories of black and white. Even in her treatment of class, there is a tendency to suggest that all white women and no black women are on the side of privilege. Poverty statistics make clear the increasing likelihood that African-American women will be in need of economic assistance programs, yet attention must be paid to differences in economic status within all racial/ethnic groups. Consideration of such particularities as sexual orientation might have pushed Thistlethwaite to consider the ways in which all communities of women are grappling with questions of differences *within* their "boundaries." The task is one of struggling to negotiate these differences without sliding into an "otherness" that continues our alienation by shifting attention away from our problematic power relationships *and* our fragile points of connection. A concept of "ambiguous multiplicity" might allow for a recognition of the many and conflicting levels of relationship that exist within and among different groups of persons while maintaining space for effective action together.

Transformation of Method: Significant transformations of theological method are evident in Thistlethwaite's text. Her starting point is a critical evaluation of the reality of white women's lives, at least white women like herself. Her sources are diverse, and she does not ghettoize literature and texts from women different from herself as "experiential" materials. Rather, all contribute to her project in general. When she returns to traditional Christian theological categories like christology and images and names for God, Thistlethwaite again incorporates diverse insights from various "voices."

Despite my criticisms of *Sex, Race, and God* — especially in my insistence that difference, and even more specific differences, cannot be the last word in any liberatory theo-ethical enterprise — Thistlethwaite's work is of critical importance in moving forward the project of decentering the exclusive focus on an authoritarian Word in light of the importance of the inclusion of multiple voices. Her insistence on holding white feminists accountable to our sources and our history, and to the liberatory potential of our work, can encourage all feminist theo-ethicists in their own attempts to develop metaphors and methodology that can further their joint commitment to the well-being of *all* women.

Along with feminist scholars in diverse disciplines, feminist theo-ethicists are increasingly conscious of the limitations of efforts to construct either theory or political practice in an exclusionary context that dismisses or ignores the experiences of most of their sisters and brothers. The works of Welch and Thistlethwaite are representative of those white feminist theologians who seek to divest themselves of the destructive legacies of their Christian heritage, in terms of both the oppression it inflicts *and* the unearned privilege it bestows, in order to participate in a more authentic theo-ethical discourse. The next step is to turn to some of the voices that have been most systematically and completely excluded from theo-ethical discourse. These voices raise unsettling questions about issues of authority and agency, the location of revelation for themselves and their communities, and the content of some primary theo-ethical categories.

Chapter 3

Voices of the Kin-dom of God

A major task for a theo-ethics of voices is that of a critical reevaluation of the locus of the revelation of God.[1] Acknowledgment of the presence of this revelation in the diverse expressions of those whose voices have not been heard in prevalent theo-ethical discourse is but a beginning point. Yet movement toward authentic dialogue with such voices is fraught with the danger of still further exploitation and misappropriation of the experiences of those with whom our relationships are characterized by inequality and oppression. The extent to which this dialogue can occur in the pages of written text — particularly text with a single author — is necessarily limited. By the use of more direct quotations than is usually the practice in written text, I signal my intention to present the "voices" I include to as great a degree as possible in their own words.

Voices of Authority and Agency

The question of authority is central to any study that engages issues of religious and/or ethical significance. How do we determine what constitutes moral action? What is the justification we give for our beliefs? What enables us to reject certain beliefs and actions as contrary to justice and integrity and to insist that others are more appropriate and life-enhancing? Our responses to any of these questions depend in large part upon our conscious or unconscious decisions about that to which we give authority. What new understandings might emerge through exploring the ways in which the diverse persons who "speak" in these pages conceive of the interaction of personal, communal, and sacred authority in their lives?

Linked to the understanding of authority in the texts under discussion here is the conception of agency. The claiming of "authority" to name one's own reality cannot be separated from the right to determine appropriate individual and communal action in response to situations of exploitation and oppression. The "theological" issues emerging from an insistence on the authority to speak in one's own voice are inherently related to the ethical issues and rights suggested by "agency." The authors of these texts refuse the imposition of rigid boundaries between thought and action and between their own agency and authority and that of God.

Given the etymology of "authority" and "agency," it is clearly appropriate to consider them together. Both come from the common Latin root *augere,* to make grow, originate, promote, increase, and its noun, *auctor,* agent. Among its definitions for "author," the *Oxford English Dictionary* lists "the person who originates or gives existence to anything: a. An inventor, constructor, or founder b. The Creator." Thus "authority" is defined both as "the power or right to enforce obedience" and also as "the power to inspire belief." The tension between these definitions lies behind my criticism of authoritarian interpretations of the Word. For the writers of the texts used as sources for the current chapter, the distinction between the two is clear. Those who embody the first definition, and who must use unjust power to enforce obedience, are clearly identified as the oppressors. The women whose stories inhabit these pages might "obey" coercive authority in order to protect themselves and their community from destruction, but they know that what carries genuine "authority" is that which has "the power to inspire belief." This applies not just to any belief but to those beliefs that motivate the people to hope for a better life for themselves and their children, beliefs that enhance their own sense of agency, of authorship of their own lives.[2]

Nobel Peace Prize recipient Rigoberta Menchú describes the receiving of this authority, located in the history of her Guatemalan Quiché Indian community, on her tenth birthday. "[The community] gave me the freedom to do what I wanted with my life as long as, first and foremost, I obeyed the laws of our ancestors. That's when they taught me not to abuse my own dignity — both as a woman and a member of our race."[3] Throughout Menchú's narrative, the "laws of the ancestors" are brought into dialogue with the violent oppression of her people as well as with the Catholic faith that her people have embraced. There is no conflict for Menchú in selecting those parts of Christianity, in its Roman Catholic representation, that are in accord with the laws of the ancestors and in rejecting those elements that support the oppressors. The authority to make those determinations lies with the community, past and present, as does the agency to act upon them.[4]

A word of caution is in order here, to avoid romanticizing the context in which communities struggling for justice gain particular wisdom and knowledge. Just as women who appear in print should not be considered "representative" of their people, neither should acknowledgment of a strong core of self-affirmation and dignity in these women minimize the personal cost of years or centuries of degradation and violation. Not all members of exploited communities maintain the level of strength exhibited by those whose words have found expression in published texts, yet neither are the strength and empowerment achieved in maintaining a sense of self necessarily greater in women who write or tell their stories for publication than they are in those who do the myriad other creative tasks through which women struggle for survival. But the power and determination of women to speak the truth of their lives, not only to those with whom they interact daily but also to a wider audience, *do* reflect their inner strength and conviction that they have something of importance to communicate. In light of the societal, cultural, and religious forces mitigating against a healthy sense of self for any other than those considered "normative" and of greatest value in the society, the strength of this sense of self-affirmation may seem more remarkable than the content of what is expressed. The resilient strength of women, however expressed, lies at the root of the survival of whole peoples and is integrally related to the claiming of authority and agency. Claiming the power and strength to speak, name, and write the experiences of one's personal and communal life cannot be separated from other political action in the world. This claim to authorship is a significant movement of strength and agency indicative of a sense of authority derived from that which has the power to inspire belief.

Claiming the Authority to Speak

Perhaps nowhere is the determination to speak, and the insistence on an authority of inspiration rather than coercion, more explicitly manifest than in the spiritual autobiographies of African-American women preachers. Women such as Jarena Lee describe a call so powerful that she and her sisters overcame powerful barriers of both race and sex in their insistence that they must speak. Lee describes her initial approach to Rev. Richard Allen, "preacher in charge of the African Society," after she could no longer deny the inner call to preach, and describes Allen's response:

As to women preaching, he said that our Discipline knew nothing at all about it — that it did not call for women preachers. This I was glad to hear, because it removed the fear of the cross — but... no sooner did this feeling cross my mind, than I found that a love of souls had in a measure departed from me; that holy energy which burned within me, as a fire, began to be smothered....

O how careful ought we to be, lest through our by-laws of church government and discipline, we bring into disrepute even the word of life. For as unseemly as it may appear now-a-days for a woman to preach, it should be remembered that nothing is impossible with God. And why should it be thought impossible, heterodox, or improper, for a woman to preach? seeing the Saviour died for the woman as well as the man.

If a man may preach, because the Saviour died for him, why not the woman? seeing he died for her also. Is he not a whole Saviour, instead of a half one? as those who hold it wrong for a woman to preach, would seem to make it appear.[5]

Although Lee's initial response is one of relief, she soon realizes that the violation of her authentic sense of call leads to feelings of distress and a lack of well-being. In addition, she engages in what today would be called a social analysis of the authorities' response, concluding with a remarkably insightful statement that is yet to be surpassed in contemporary arguments for women's ordination. Lee affirms her original call and goes on to act upon it, while at the same time refuting the authority of those who insist that it is not her place to preach.

Zilpha Elaw has a similar response to those who attempt to legislate against her own call to preach. Elaw is aware that the words of St. Paul are used to deny the function of preaching to women, yet she insists:

It is true, that in the ordinary course of Church arrangement and order, the Apostle Paul laid it down as a rule, that females should not speak in the church, nor be suffered to teach; but the Scriptures make it evident that this rule was not intended to limit the extraordinary directions of the Holy Ghost, in reference to female Evangelists, or oracular sisters; nor to be rigidly observed in peculiar circumstances.[6]

Elaw notes women such as Phoebe, who were clearly active in Paul's time, and suggests that it was particular excesses in the church of that day that motivated the apostle to write as he did. Although the scriptures are important to Elaw, she is clear that the words were indeed written by men for a particular time and place and that the voice of the

Spirit must take precedence. Speaking of her reception by a Methodist preacher, she notes, " 'We do not allow,' sounded very uncouthly in my ears in a matter in which the commission of the Almighty is assumed."[7] Elaw's own relationship with God is primary in determining authority for her preaching ministry.

Julia Foote describes her delight in learning basic literacy skills. "Imagine, if you can, my childish glee over this, my first lesson. The children of the present time...can not realize my joy at being able to say the entire alphabet when I was nine years old."[8] Like Elaw and Lee, Foote encounters resistance when she attempts to implement her call to preach. Aware of the double standard pertaining to men and women, she maintains that "a woman will be believed when she shows credentials from heaven," meaning the accomplishment of a miracle. But, insists Foote, "[I]f it be necessary to prove one's right to preach the Gospel, I ask of my brethren to show me their credentials, or I can not believe in the propriety of their ministry."[9] Again, self-asserted male authority is challenged in the face of the belief of these women that their own call comes from elsewhere and is not to be denied.

Women such as Lee, Elaw, and Foote are sometimes criticized, along with their white mystic sisters such as Julian of Norwich and Hildegard of Bingen, for imputing all "authority" to God, to the detriment of their own sense of personal agency. The autobiography of Alabama midwife Onnie Lee Logan suggests that many women do not maintain the dualism often present in the work of white, Western, masculinist theologians between God and self. For Logan, God's authority and *her* authority are coterminous. Logan describes taking midwife classes in order to be licensed under new laws in Alabama:

> I can only put it this way and I can be for sho that I'm right. Two-thirds of what I know about deliverin, carin for mother and baby, what to expect, what was happenin and was goin on, I didn't get it from the class. *God gave it to me. So many things I got from my own plain motherwit.*[10]

God's gifts and her own motherwit are not described as two different realities by Logan. A sense of competence and confidence pervades her story, not least in her determination that her life experiences should be told. "I got so much experience in here that I just want to explode," she told her "collaborator." "I want to show that I knew what I knew — I want somebody to realize what I am."[11] Later, in describing how she treated her patients to "keep em from tearin," she notes that she's "letting out one a my secrets. I don't want to bury em. There's so much that I don't want to die with.... That's what gave me the idea to do a book."[12]

The two women who are the key "characters" in Kathleen Hirsch's *Songs from the Alley,* a study of homelessness in Boston, have a different but related experience of asserting their right to speak and be heard.[13] These are not women who had education refused them in their early years, yet their early life contexts, and tensions and abuse within their families of origin, leave both Wendy and Amanda alone and feeling abandoned and isolated as they attempt to build some kind of life for themselves. Neither Wendy nor Amanda mentions God or any religious "authority," yet both women maintain the capacity to claim a certain *personal* authority that the violence in their lives cannot totally extinguish. Wendy eschews the shelter system for the restrictions that would be imposed on her life, while for Amanda, the shelter and the persons she comes to know there provide greater freedom than did her family.

Both of these women need to affirm their sense of self by expressing their reality in a way that can be shared. In a brief respite from the alcohol-induced daze in which Wendy passes much of her time, she begins a journal. She titles her first entry "Do I Care?"

> I doubt that I can call this a short story or essay. Nor can I expect anyone to understand this brief account of one of the many steps toward my self destruction. Someday I hope to write down the alpha and maybe the possible omega of it all.... Maybe, someday, I'll be able to tell of the past ten years of horrendous hell and self torture ... I have continued to live in my own destructive and defeated fashion. But do I really care? Tell me. Do I?[14]

By the end of Hirsch's narrative, Wendy is still on the streets, still drinking, still not at the point she only tentatively imagines in her writing. Yet even in her despair, Wendy can glimpse and *record* the possibility of reclaiming her own agency. In fact, she acknowledges in her words that even the "destructive and defeated fashion" in which she lives is to a considerable extent the result of her own actions and choices. As Wendy comments, "[U]pstanding citizens regard us street people as human garbage. But I know far more loving and caring people who exist on the streets."[15]

Keeping a journal is a more directly empowering activity for Amanda, who "chooses" the shelter system as the one context where she can find access to some of the support and services she knows she needs. Amanda speaks fondly of a drop-in center that offers lunch and a quiet place where she can sit and write. The staff at the shelter where she sleeps also encourage her "to the point that an old ambition of hers, to become a writer, has been rekindled."[16] The theft of Amanda's notebook is a major tragedy, deterring her for a time. An insight into her own *choice* to remain on the streets, at least for a while, eventually leads Amanda back to her writing. What she realizes is that she does not want a home "until having a home can be a positive experience" and that "this concept is next to impossible to convey to someone on the outside, someone with a home looking out on those without." Amanda begins a poem: "Boston, we are your street people, your homeless.... We are your father, your husband, your mother, your wife, your son, your daughter, your run-away teen-ager."[17] Amanda writes as she has never written before, losing all sense of time, and by the time she returns to the shelter that evening, she is ready to approach a counselor and ask for help. Eventually this self-chosen connection with counselor Jackie will provide Amanda with the support she needs to begin to develop an identity other than that of a homeless woman.

Any organized religious activity experienced by Amanda and Wendy has led them to view religion with deep suspicion. Yet these women draw on a strength of connection with their own deepest longings and yearnings and with those persons who touch their lives with kindness and authentic engagement, as they insist that their lives are important and that they have something to say that others may want and need to hear.

Claiming Agency in the Choice of Expression

If the strength and authority to claim the right to speak/write are central to women's survival, so too is the ability to determine the form and language in which such expression will take place. Women and others from oppressed communities have consistently manipulated the languages imposed upon them in ways that have made those languages more adequate to express their own lived experiences. Although the significance of the genre of imaginative fiction/fantasy/science fiction as a resource for theo-ethical discourse is taken up in the next chapter, one significant example of this style of literature illuminates the way in which the choice of alternative modes of communication enables diverse voices to speak in their own tongues. Linguist Suzette Haden Elgin has chosen this medium to demonstrate the power of language and the need of oppressed peoples to create their own linguistic systems to communicate those experiences for which there are no adequate expressions in the "master" tongue. Elgin discusses the basic hypothesis that underlies her insights as a linguist — that of the power of language to change and reconstruct social reality — and her decision to explore this hypothesis through the medium of imaginative fiction:

> What I want is to get the exploration of this hypothesis not into the hands of a hundred scientists but out before the public, and the bigger the public the better....Ideally an article in *Family Circle* and an article in *TV Guide;* but I don't have the skills for that sort of journalism and I don't have the reputation. Science fiction, on the other hand, I do have a certain amount of entry to. So I decided to do it as a science fiction novel and the novel would take up the hypothesis that...language does become a mechanism for social change. And it would explore the hypothesis that existing human languages, and English in particular, are inadequate to express the perceptions of women. And it would explore the hypothesis that if you were to introduce into American culture a language that did express the perceptions of women, that culture would perforce self-destruct and change radically. *Native Tongue* is the result.[18]

In her science fiction series, Elgin portrays a future time in which defeat of the Equal Rights Amendment has left women under rigid control of the males in their lives.[19] The exploration and colonization of planets with alien populations have led to a shift of power in which a particular set of families has control of the technologies necessary to "interface" human infants with humanoid aliens in order to allow transference of their linguistic capacities and thus enable communication between them. The women of these "linguist" families are the ones who recognize the potential of language to change social reality and who have the skills to embark upon an ambitious project of language construction that will express women's experiences in ways inaccessible through current language patterns.

Because of her profession, Elgin is deeply aware of the power of language, so much so that she developed the language of Láadan herself prior to introducing it in her novels:

> I was proposing that a language had been constructed deliberately by women and for women with the goal of bringing about drastic social change....I felt that it was my ethical obligation before I wrote the novel to work up the language so that I could see what kind of problems you would run into and what sort of insights there would be, and so that I would have a context from within which to write the book.[20]

Adopting the "silent and subtle"[21] approach common to many of their foresisters, Elgin's female characters devise a two-tier structure to their language. The first, Langlish, is an ornately clumsy construction that successfully masks the deeper structural development of Láadan itself. Langlish is seen by the men as some harmless project of the women that keeps them busy and happy and thus less bothersome. In the "Manual for Beginners," the fictional developers of Láadan explain the difference:

> The linguistic term *lexical encoding* refers to the way that human beings choose a particular chunk of their world, external or internal, and assign that chunk a surface chunk that will be its name; it refers to the process of word-making. When we women say "Encoding," with a capital "E," we mean something a little bit different. We mean the making of a name for a chunk of the world that so far as we know has never been made or found or dumped upon your culture. We mean naming a chunk that has been around a long time but has never before impressed anyone as sufficiently important to *deserve* its own name.[22]

Not surprisingly, many of the experiences that have not been deemed worthy of a name are those most common to the women. Thus *lowitheláad* means "to feel, as if directly, another's pain/grief/surprise/joy/anger," and *ráahedethi* means "to be unable to feel *lowitheláad*, to be empathically impaired"; *ráahedethilh* also means "empathically impaired," but in the sense of being *unwilling* to feel *lowitheláad*.[23]

After many years of developing the vocabulary and grammatical guidelines for Láadan, the women decide that the time is right to begin using it with girl children. Within a short time, the women notice a heightened sense of delight in the children and an increased degree of closeness among them. Some older women reflect poignantly upon the empowerment of having a language that accurately reflects one's reality:

> "Well, no wonder they are so knit together, then," Nazareth observed. "Remember that some of them have had that blissful resource from the day they were born."
>
> "I cannot imagine it," Grace said emphatically. "I try, but I can't. What that must be like. Not to be always groping, because there aren't any words — while the person you want so desperately to talk to gets tired of waiting and begins talking of something else. To have a language that works, that says what you want to say easily and efficiently, and to have *always* had that? No, loves, I cannot imagine it. I am too old."[24]

The dominating language of any society may be grossly inadequate for communicating the full meaning of the lives of many people within the society. Jeannette Armstrong, a Canadian Okanagan Indian, speaks of the conflict she experienced within her family, particularly in terms of the practice in both Canada and the United States of taking First Nations children into residential schools in which they were forbidden to speak their native languages. Her grandmother refused to speak English at all and "refused to allow my father and my uncles and my sisters to receive any sort of white education, in any way."[25] Armstrong's father, on the other hand, came to realize that he must speak the oppressor's language for his own and his family's survival. The value both of maintaining her own language and of learning English well becomes clear to Armstrong. Yet she is also aware of "the value of having a grandmother who could speak to me in the total purity of our language," a purity not adulterated by exposure to English.[26] Rejecting the Christianity that motivated those who were responsible for the colonization of her people, Armstrong describes the strong connections she experiences between the spirituality of her community and the language with which they communicate and think about the world in which they live:

> Spirituality is very, very clearly tied in with my purpose of being, as an Okanagan woman, born into this world at this time. I am still searching for my own purpose, but I understand I have been given an ability to speak two languages, to cross between these two languages in my mind. I also understand that our language comes from a sacred place. I don't understand where the English language originates, yet, but when Native people think about the source of thought we consider the vast pool of creation and its origin. We think about the things that formed us as thinking, human, walking people, different from the animal people. When we consider the spiritual place from which our thinking arises, the words become sacred things because they come from that place. My responsibility is to strive for correctness in my presentation, correctness of purpose and accuracy in my use of words in my attempt to transcend the simple actuality of the things I have seen, to the image of those same things in the context of my entire history and the sacred body of knowledge that we, as a people, have acquired.[27]

Right language is crucial to the full expression of culture and spirituality. Paula Gunn Allen, a Laguna Pueblo/Sioux literary critic, notes that thought and intelligence are at the heart of that with which the Great Spirit has endowed all in the tribe. The authority to create language and to determine its modes of expression is shared between this Great Spirit and the community, as cocreators:

The purpose of traditional American Indian literature is never simply pure self-expression.... The tribes seek — through song, ceremony, legend, sacred stories (myths), and tales — to embody, articulate, and share reality, to bring the isolated private self into harmony and balance with this reality, to verbalize the sense of the majesty and reverent mystery of all things, and to actualize, in language, those truths that give to humanity its greatest significance and dignity.[28]

For Allen, as for Armstrong, the voices of the people and the expressive language they use are intrinsically related to the Spirit from which life flows and that gives meaning to the universe in which they live.

Most African-Americans in the United States do not retain the same connection with the original languages spoken by their people as do Armstrong and Allen. Yet neither have they merely taken on standard English. The coercive authority of the dominating societal structures has resulted in a denial of the integrity of Black English by "educated" members of the society, yet the authenticity and strength of this language have been amply demonstrated by numerous works of African-American authors.[29] Geneva Smitherman uses W. E. B. du Bois's concept of "double consciousness" to indicate the dilemma African-Americans have faced in having to develop the capacity to communicate in White English in order to participate at any level in dominating societal structures, while retaining Black English for use in their communities. As a linguist participating in civil rights court cases involving issues of education for African-American children, Smitherman is aware of the contemporary problem. The language that most adequately articulates such children's reality — Black English — is considered "unsuitable" in formal educational and political contexts that have insisted upon so-called standard English and have thus functioned to educate children "away from — not toward — Black culture, language, and community."[30] Smitherman links this factor with the high level of "functional illiteracy" currently documented among black children. Cynically, but all too accurately, she claims that "from the perspective of the state, this is as it should be. After all, if the niggers become literate, they just might read the handwriting on the wall."[31]

Yet even in the face of overwhelming odds, Black English has developed and survived in ways that Smitherman insists must be acknowledged as genuine "language" and not merely a dialect of English. Enslaved peoples, brought to this country and deliberately scattered in terms of their original ethnic-language groups, still managed to forge a new language that enabled them to share with one another "*in* the oppressor's language" while not becoming a part *of* it. Such language, says Smitherman, "became a source of power because the Africanized style of speaking was fully understood only by those born under the threat of the lash."[32] Because of the deep structure of this language, Black English cannot adequately be characterized as a "dialect" of White English. If the term "language" is correctly understood, as incorporating "the history and social rules that govern the use, production, and interpretation of the words, grammar, and sounds," Black English must be considered a language in its own right.[33]

The need to survive in the dominating culture leads to a dilemma for peoples struggling to maintain their own authenticity through retention of their own language, as noted by Armstrong and others above. June Jordan describes the ambivalent reaction of her students to reading Alice Walker's *The Color Purple*. In speech reflective of Celie's language in the text, Jordan's students criticized Walker's use of "Black English" as inappropriate. Jordan uses this occasion to engage her students in an examination of the ways in which they have been disempowered through the derogation of their own language and modes of expression. Jordan's realization of the degree to which her students had unconsciously accepted the culture's criticism of their own modes of expression, and their excitement over being empowered to affirm their own language, led to her developing a class in Black English in which she and her students began the process of examining the structure and patterns of the language that most of them had spoken most of their lives. Jordan describes her own concerns that the values associated with Black English should not be lost:

> We begin to grow up in a house where every true mirror shows us the face of somebody who does not belong there, whose walk and whose talk will never look or sound "right," because that house was meant to shelter a family that is alien and hostile to us. As we learn our way around this environment, either we hide our original word habits, or we completely surrender our own voice, hoping to please those who will never respect anyone different from themselves: Black English is not exactly a linguistic buffalo, but we should understand its status as an endangered species, as a perishing, irreplaceable system of community intelligence, or we should expect its extinction, and, along with that, the extinguishing of much that constitutes our own proud, and singular identity.[34]

With Jordan's "permission," the students reclaimed their *own* authority to articulate their perceptions of truth in their authentic voices. During the course of her class, a brother of one of Jordan's students was shot and killed by the police. Members of her Black English class decided to express their outrage by writing to both media and police officials in their newly reclaimed tongue, despite their awareness that this would render unlikely publication of, or action in response to, their letters. Having recognized themselves as authentically bilingual, Jordan's students were able to determine which language was more adequate to express their reality in any given situation.

Claiming the Truth in Oral-Aural Wisdom

The dilemma encountered by Jordan and her students, and many of those whose lives are inadequately reflected in the language they must use to engage the dominating society, is reflective of a rigid compartmentalization of what constitutes knowledge. A key component in this division is a perceived polarization between "truth" and oral-aural wisdom. I have discussed the gradual historical displacement of concepts of Sophia/Wisdom by static and rigid interpretations of Logos/Word. As this Word became more and more associated with text, and thus the property of an elite, educated, clerical caste, Wisdom was devalued and "reduced" to such notions as "intuition" and "instinct." Yet these very qualities have enabled whole communities and nations of people to survive against centuries of violence and exploitation. Given the current potential of the so-called developed world to destroy all life on the planet through ecological and/or nuclear devastation, a better case might be made against some of the "achievements" of scientific knowledge than against the wisdom of devalued peoples.

Reclaiming the authority of this wisdom is the urgent task of many African-American scholars and activists. In her study of black women's literature and its contributions to a black womanist ethic, Katie Geneva Cannon insists that these novelists, while not formally "historians, sociologists, nor theologians," nevertheless reflect in their work "historical facts, sociological realities and religious convictions that lie behind the ethos and ethics of the Black community."[35] Cannon goes on to note that black women writers manage to capture in their work both the truth of the current realities of their communities and also the wisdom of generations that has empowered their survival:

> Black women writers document the attitudes and morality of women, men, girls, and boys who chafe at and defy the restrictions imposed by the dominant white-capitalist value system. They delineate in varying artistic terms the folk treasury of the Black community, in terms of how Black people deal with pov-

erty and the ramifications of power, sex as an act of love and terror, the depersonalization that accompanies violence, the acquisition of property, the drudgery of a workday, the inconsistencies of chameleon-like racism, teenage mothers, charlatan sorcerers, swinging churches, stoic endurance and stifled creativity. Out of this storehouse of Black experiences comes a "vitally rich, ancient continuum" of Black wisdom.[36]

This writing "can be trusted as seriously mirroring Black reality" and provides "*truthful* interpretations of every possible shade and nuance of Black life."[37] There is no clear distinction between wisdom and truth, because truth, like wisdom, is not a static, reified object. The phrase "truthful interpretations" implies an approach to "truth" that is more akin to the understandings of wisdom related to Sophia. There is no "thing" called truth; rather, truthful interpretations emerge as the community and its chroniclers share historical and contemporary stories of day-to-day survival, hopes and dreams, fears and limitations.

Those whose voices speak in this chapter who consider themselves "Christian" have a sense of the authority of the Bible or whatever church institution they affiliate with that is very different from that delineated in Protestant biblicism and Roman Catholic magisterialism. These women, and those who do not claim a religious context, struggle to bring that which comes from their own ancestral heritage and that which is imported from outside into critical engagement with their own contemporary situation in determining what will be considered authoritative. Whether the experience is named in religious terms or not, the capacity to speak in the language and voices most organic to one's own community contributes centrally to owning and claiming authority and agency.

Voices of Revelation

The determination of the women quoted above to claim their own authority to speak the truth of their lives in the language that best expresses that reality demonstrates powerful resistance to societal and cultural forces that demand silence and capitulation. This spoken and written expression is most often integrally related with other actions of resistance in the service of individual and communal survival and raises theo-ethical concerns that have been either neglected by the white, Western theological enterprise or pronounced upon without the participation of those most in a position to speak authoritatively. I focus here on two major traditional theological categories: the recognition and naming of what constitutes sin and grace, and understandings of salvation and the kin-dom of God. Many of the women whose lives and words inform this exploration may not identify with those terms. My point in using them is to demonstrate the radical rethinking that must take place — including the possible renaming of many of what have been considered to be central Christian theological tenets — when we consider seriously the diverse insights that emerge from multiple locations.

Sin and Grace

In the film *Sorceress,* a representative of the Spanish Inquisition arrives in a small French feudal town to investigate reports of a heretical woman who is practicing witchcraft. Her "crime" is that of healing the villagers through the herbal remedies that have been passed on to her from generations of women in her family. The inquisitor meets a peasant who is working at the side of the road and inquires of him if he has heard anything of a heretic in the area. The peasant replies that indeed he has: the lord of the manor makes all his serfs work night and day for barely enough food to feed their children; he takes all the profits and kicks and beats his workers if they don't comply with his every whim. This interaction encapsulates the different understandings of evil/ sin held by those who represent biblicist or magisterialist positions and others who see from a different perspective.

The capacity of exploited women to "name the enemy" and to identify accurately what constitutes "sin" for them and their people is of major significance to their exercise of agency. Onnie Lee Logan discusses the high incidence of infant mortality in Alabama and the resulting regulation of midwives. Logan asserts:

> The midwife was blamed. That was not the midwife. That was the lackin of prenatal care. No vitamins, no calciums. No prenatal care whatsoever. It was not havin the proper food. Not havin enough calcium for her and baby.... It wasn't because of the midwives. They had to lay the situation on somebody and so they laid it on the midwives.[38]

Logan *knows* what causes high infant mortality rates and refuses the assignment of responsibility to the midwives and "the ones that wasn't midwives that knowed how to do work."[39] Marjorie Bard records the words of a homeless woman who likewise refuses to accept blame for the circumstances beyond her control that have left her without housing and other resources:

If any of the men I talked to had taken me seriously, I wouldn't have lost all of my money. I had to sell the house fast and didn't get very much. Then I went into a depression. Almost all of the money from the sale of the house went for a stay in a clinic, and now I don't have anything at all. I don't feel well enough to start looking for a job, and I don't know what I'd do.

If a man went into any of the places I did and told the same story, I'll bet he'd have help right away.[40]

Lois, the woman interviewed by Bard, has experienced the police and Legal Aid representatives she has approached as invested in upholding the same system that has allowed her husband to manipulate her out of her own financial resources. The "authorities" were not interested in hearing what she had to say, with the result that Larry got away with her money and she ended up on the streets.

Jesus' command that we should love our enemies might be interpreted to include the need to first be able to name them. Identification of the real causes of the oppression under which people suffer, including the identity of those who are the individual agents of that suffering, is central to conceptions of sin that place guilt where it belongs and not wrongfully upon those who are the recipients of violence and exploitation. The ability to make this identification accurately is a prerequisite for the "grace" uncovered in resistance struggles that refuse the authority of oppressive structures.

Rigoberta Menchú counts the moments of this identification of sin as integral to her own empowerment in her struggles for the survival of her Quiché people. Initially, Menchú's awareness focuses on recognition that the tragedies she experiences — for example the death from malnutrition of her little brother on the *finca* where her family was working — were not the work of "fate." "Those fifteen days working in the *finca* was one of my earliest experiences and I remember it with enormous hatred. That hatred has stayed with me until today."[41] Menchú takes on the responsibility of educating the community:

> It was my job to explain to the children of the community that our situation had nothing to do with fate but was something which had been imposed on us.... The rich have become rich because they took what our ancestors had away from them, and now they grow fat on the sweat of our labour.[42]

Identifying the individuals who are directly responsible for her own and her people's suffering leads Menchú into articulation of the structural problems that must be overcome and into recognition that not *all ladinos* are receiving benefits from the exploitative system:

Little by little, I discovered many ways in which we had to be understanding towards our *ladino* friends and in which they had to show us understanding too. Because I also knew *compañeros ladinos* with whom we shared the worst conditions, but who still felt *ladino,* and as *ladinos* they didn't see that our poverty united us. But little by little, both they and I began discussing many very important things and saw that the root of our problems lay in the ownership of the land. All our country's riches are in the hands of the few.[43]

Land ownership thus becomes the issue that must be addressed on every level if the Indian peoples of Guatemala are ever to have a better life. Similarly, Hortensia, a Salvadoran woman interviewed by Renny Golden, insists on an accurate naming of the causes of *her* people's suffering:

We have suffered because we demanded our rights — simply for thinking it was unjust to leave our children and to work for a minimum wage from sunup to sundown. That's the origin of our rebellion — simply that. The poor majority simply asked that we share in what the minority has gained through our labor and sweat.[44]

Watching her brother tortured and savagely murdered became the catalyst for Menchú to name the means by which land ownership is retained by the wealthy few as "sin":

Indians are already being killed off by malnutrition, and when our parents can hardly give us enough to live on, and make such sacrifices so that we can grow up, then they burn us alive like that. Savagely. I said, this is impossible, and that was precisely the moment for me, personally, when I finally felt firmly convinced that if it's a sin to kill a human being, how can what the regime does to us not be a sin?[45]

For Menchú's mother, too, this moment was one in which she made the decision to fight in every way possible to overcome the regime that was responsible for the suffering, a commitment that would cost her an excruciatingly tortured death. "When a woman sees her son tortured and burned to death, she is incapable of forgiving anyone or ridding herself of that hatred, that bitterness. . . . She took this important message and was very influential in many places."[46]

Yet as Menchú's words about the *ladinos* indicate, she is aware of the danger of a simplistic designation of "enemy" that fails to consider the limitations of her own people and the possibility for redemptive characteristics in others. Octavia Butler discusses this complexity as she has developed the theme in her science fiction novels:

> There are a lot of people (unfortunately, some of them are writers and editors) who seem to see things strictly in terms of good and evil: the aliens either come to help us get our poor heads straightened out or they come to destroy us. What I hope to wind up with in my work are a series of shadings that correspond to the way concepts like "good" and "evil" enter into the real world — never absolute, always by degrees. In my novels, generally, everybody wins and loses something... because as I see it, that's pretty much the way the world is.[47]

Whether it be the immortals Doro and Anyanwu in *Wild Seed* or Dana and Kevin, black woman and white man unwillingly transported back in time to an 1815 Maryland plantation in *Kindred,* Butler's characters defy easy personification of good and evil.[48]

If sin lies in those who have exploited and abused Menchú's people for five hundred years, grace may well lie in determination to resist the oppression itself and to resist attempts to "Christianize" their response in terms of the mandate to "love." The particular activities that emerge from the validation/authorization of this analysis will vary as widely as the people involved, particularly in relationship to the immediacy of the threat to survival. Living with the threat of psychological control imposed through both surgery and medication, Elgin's linguist women use the "subtle and silent" approach, along with their clear analysis of the men's ways of being, to gradually insinuate Láadan into the language of their society. The "outsider" woman who is hired as a nurse is never told anything directly about the "Encoding Project," yet she too begins to absorb the strategies used by the linguists:

> She was watching him as she spoke, watching for that subtle change in his expression that would mean she was going too far and he was about to realize that she was putting him on. But he seemed genuinely pleased — unless he was putting *her* on.... [D]id he have that much imagination? She saw no signs of suspicion. It was astonishing how easily a man could be made to believe you when you were saying exactly what he wanted you to say, no matter how improbable it was. And she realized suddenly that before she had come here and lived among the Chornyak women she had not suspected that for an instant. She had learned that here, without even realizing that she was learning. Strange — and very welcome.[49]

Women whose entire communities are physically threatened in terms of their very survival may not have the same opportunity to select an approach that relies upon subtle manipulation over a long period of time. This marks a major difference in resistance strategies between groups that are needed by the dominating society and are thus targeted for exploitation and those that are considered expendable and may be targeted for genocide. Yet for all exploited women, some measure of grace is the result of the accurate naming of the forces of oppression marshaled against them, grace made most visibly manifest in communal action in the service of survival.

Diverse and creative modes of resistance mean that change may happen almost imperceptibly. Lee Maracle realizes that the claiming of her own language *and* English has been a source of empowerment that, while not enabling Canadian First Nations people to achieve the full rights they seek, has nevertheless allowed some significant advances. Maracle listens as her young daughter makes a phone call:

> "Hello, Tim Horton's Donuts? I am inquiring about your advertisement for a job. Yes. Is it still available? It is. Well asshole, why did you tell me it was filled!" She hangs up and starts looking up the Human Rights Commission number. I did not fix the world for her like I promised twenty years ago, but I did change something. Silence. Passive resistance is no longer our way of being. I watch her. Like me she is fighting back.[50]

Voice and resistance action, for Maracle and her daughter, are integrally related.

No treatment of resistance is complete without some mention of the issue of violence. The question of forceful resistance, to the point of violent self-defense, is a troublesome one in feminist theo-ethical discourse, as in much Christian theology. Self-defense becomes a central concern for Rigoberta Menchú, as the military engage increasingly in acts of violence against villages throughout Guatemala. There is a clear distinction in the minds of Menchú and her community between any glorification of martyrdom and the knowledge that action on behalf of one's community may lead to death. The fundamental concern is always the survival of the community, a commitment that comes before personal safety. The preservation of life, of all life, is sought wherever possible and by whatever means are necessary. If taking up arms in self-defense is the only way to protect the community from obliteration, then self-defense is graced action in response to the sin of the military assassins. Before he leaves to embark upon the activities that will lead ultimately to his own death, Menchú's father shares some advice with his family:

Some people give their blood and some people give their strength. So while we can, we must give our strength. In this hour of need, we must look after our little lives very well so that they provide a source of strength for our people.... We want no more dead, we want no more martyrs, because we already have too many in our land, in our fields, through too many massacres. What we must do is protect our lives as much as we can and carry on with our struggle.[51]

These words are reminiscent of the premise of Delores Williams — that *survival* is the primary metaphor in African-American women's appropriation of biblical texts.[52]

Comandante Rebeca Palacios, of El Salvador's Farabundo Martí National Liberation Front (FMLN),[53] speaks of her participation in the resistance struggle of her people as "one of the greatest joys I've ever known."[54] Much of the joy experienced by Palacios has been engendered by her witnessing of the powerful survival determination of her people:

Basically, my confidence, my faith, the convictions that I have, are rooted in the fact that the Salvadoran people have shown that they are no longer willing to be anybody's slave. The people have an immense longing for democracy and the people themselves are mobilizing, with more initiative, with more enthusiasm, to struggle for basic social transformations. So if my people, an illiterate, poor, underdeveloped people, have this kind of spirit to keep on struggling and moving forward, in spite of what has been done to them, in spite of the bombings, in spite of the massacres, in spite of all who have been "disappeared," if seventy-eight thousand victims are not sufficient to make this people quit, then I have absolute confidence that this people has the moral and material strength capable of changing the destiny of our country.[55]

And, one might add, in spite of the millions of dollars of U.S. aid that has gone into supporting the government against the member organizations of the FMLN and the peasant populations that support them.

Again, many of the women who speak here of their participation in the resistance struggles of their people are not Christian, indeed make no reference to any religious foundation for their action. Yet some do claim a Christian or other religious tradition, not as granting any ultimate authority, but rather as something that provides a resource for the development of their own authority and agency. Rigoberta Menchú, in

speaking of her own dawning awareness of the need for her community to arm itself in preparation for self-defense, notes that "our main
weapon [was] the Bible."[56] Of particular significance to Menchú are the
stories of Judith, Moses, and David. Moses, as one who "tried to lead
his people from oppression," and David, "a little shepherd boy...who
was able to defeat the king of those days, King Goliath," have great
power to inspire a people facing great military and political power with
nothing more than a few simple farming implements. And Judith is inspiration for the women: "She fought very hard for her people and made
many attacks against the king they had then, until she finally had his
head."[57] These texts are inspirational, authoritative in the sense of "in-
spiring belief," because they can be related so directly to everyday life.
Church representatives can fulfill a similar role to the extent that they
too can join with the people:

> We know very well that we don't need a king in a palace but a
> brother who lives with us. We don't need a leader to show us
> where God is, to say whether he exists or not, because, through
> our own conception of God, we know there is a God and that,
> as the father of us all, he does not wish even one of his chil-
> dren to die, or be unhappy, or have no joy in life. We believe
> that, when we started using the Bible, when we began studying
> it in terms of our reality, it was because we found in it a docu-
> ment to guide us. It's not that the document itself brings about the
> change.[58]

Menchú does not cast her decisions and actions in terms of theological doctrine. Yet when the voices of people such as Menchú, Logan,
Butler, Elgin, Amanda, Armstrong, Maracle and her daughter, and Palacios enter theo-ethical conversation, issues and concepts that have long
been central to white, Western theological discourse — such as sin and
grace — are shown in new perspective. The question of resistance as
grace, even when it may be violent, is a particularly volatile area that
needs sustained attention by any theo-ethicists who claim to want to
be in solidarity with their sisters and brothers in such contexts as Guatemala, El Salvador, South Africa, and many of the "homes" in our
own country. As Melanie Kaye/Kantrowitz observes, "Our choices are
not clean hands or bloody ones. The blood is already being spilled."[59]
Simplistic rejection or advocacy of violence, from those who are not
immersed in the reality of the situation, are irrelevant *and* irreverent
to a people insistent on authoring their own understandings of what
constitutes authentic theo-ethical action.

Salvation and the Kin-dom of God

Most contemporary white feminist and other liberation theologians join the women cited in this chapter in refusing an other-worldly interpretation of salvation and insist that authentic hope and faith require both movement toward and action on behalf of that "kin-dom" in *this* world. If God/sacred reality is to be considered intimately related to (and *with*) all created being — in Christian terms, incarnate — then the integrity of all life, past, present, and future, constitutes the basic criterion of salvation.

Rigoberta Menchú notes that her people "don't actually have the word God." She speaks of a sense of the one "father" who is "the heart of the sky, that is, the sun," which corresponds to the concept of God, but goes on to say that "our mother is the moon [who] lights our way" and describes the two realities as "the pillars of the universe."[60] Menchú's people experience themselves as "part of the natural world."[61] This interdependence is ever-present and visible in a community that must work in harmony with the seasons, the productivity of the land, and climatic disturbances in order to survive:

> We worship — or rather not worship but respect — a lot of things to do with the natural world, the most important things for us. For instance, to us, water is sacred.... We must only harm the earth when we are in need. This is why, before we sow our maize, we have to ask the earth's permission.[62]

Menchú speaks of Catholicism and other Christian religion having as a basic premise that "God loves the poor and has a wonderful paradise in Heaven for the poor, so the poor must accept the life they have on Earth."[63] Yet the combination of their life experiences and their own creative appropriation of biblical stories has led Menchú's people to understand all too clearly that "unless a religion springs from within the people themselves, it is a weapon of the system."[64] God is with the people who are struggling to resist and survive and supports their efforts, including their actions of self-defense. And because the available "weapons" are everyday items such as work tools, stones, soap, and hot water, a ceremony is held asking "our one God to help us and give us permission to use his creations of nature to defend ourselves with."[65]

In an understanding of the kin-dom of God as mandating action for salvation in *this* world, revelation is found in diverse places and may *not* be limited to the Bible or other specifically religious contexts. Reina, a Salvadoran regional director of Christian base communities who has been forced underground because of her activities, speaks of the source

of revelation of her own "call" to give herself over totally to the cause
of the Salvadoran people:

> Some still believe this,... that this is a direct call from God. But
> I believe you shouldn't make such an unquestioning affirmation.
> Why couldn't we better say that it's a call from our fellow human
> beings?[66]

Venancia, a catechist, has a similar sense of just where God's revelation
is located:

> I've discovered the gospel more. Not perhaps in the Bible so much,
> but in each *compañero,* in each brother and sister that is here
> struggling day and night for life. Each of them testifies to the
> gospel that Christ speaks about in the Bible. And this is what fills
> us with conviction and faith and hope that we are going to achieve
> this new society, which is a path toward what Christians desire
> most, the Reign of God.[67]

Salvation comes, for these women, in responding to God's call *in* the
call of their people.

If God's call comes from the people among whom one lives and
works, then coercive authority structures do not have the right to deny
or to attempt to revoke that "call." Onnie Lee Logan appeals directly to
God's commands when she responds to the eventual phasing out of the
licensing of midwives in Alabama:

> They're not gonna stop me from doin the gift that God give me
> to do. The Lord hadn't quite give me the answer but all I'm sayin
> is that God don't aim for me with the experience He give me and
> the talent He gave me, He don't aim for me to let man, white nor
> black, kill it unless my health failed on me.... I don't need a permit
> to deliver no babies. If God tell me not to do it I won't do it.[68]

Again Logan does not differentiate between what God tells her to do
and her own "motherwit." Using the gifts she has for the good of her
community, and for as long as her health will permit, is Logan's primary
commitment. One can infer that her response to any church official who
stepped in to command her compliance would receive a response similar
to those given by the women preachers cited above!

The road to the kin-dom lies in authentic recognition and following
of God's revelation. Japanese Canadian novelist and poet Joy Kogawa
also suggests that "salvation" inheres in wholehearted response to that
which calls most deeply:

What matters is that you listen to the voice that calls you, whether it comes from the bottom of the well, or whether it comes from the distant stars, whether it comes from your community, whether it comes from within your own heart, whether it comes from your neighbour or from your mate, or whomever it comes from, your calling is to respond to the voice that calls you. Fundamentally, that response is the response of love, so the writer's role is no different than any other human being's role, which is fundamentally to love and to respond to the voice that cries out to you.[69]

"Saving one's soul" is not a concept that occurs to these women. In fact, as Menchú noted, religion that has such a focus does not come from the depths of the people and can only serve to support the structures of oppression against which her community struggles.

If salvation cannot be conceived of as something for which to hope only in some future time, neither is it interpreted as an individual reality. Korean theologian Chung Hyun Kyung insists that for Asian women the very reality of God is understood as a community rather than as an individual. Therefore no individual, but only the community in its relationships among members, can image God:

In this image of God as the community in relationship, there is no place for only one, solitary, all-powerful God who sits on the top of the hierarchical power pyramid and dominates all other living beings. Where there is no mutual relationship, there is no human experience of God. Asian women emphasize the importance of community in their theologies because only in community can humanity reflect God and fulfill the image of God in which we were created for mutual relationship.[70]

For Brazilian theologian María Clara Bingemer, an understanding of God as relational is an invitation to reflect on the Christian concept of the Trinity. This doctrine, suggests Bingemer, has the potential to express that "God is a community of love between persons...where the differences and pluralities are not suppressed but integrated."[71]

The centrality of the importance of community pervades Menchú's book, and her life. She describes how a new baby is welcomed into the community, that the child "belongs to the community not just to the parents,"[72] and that "the baby's school must be the community itself, that he must learn to live like all the rest of us."[73] Despite the hardships encountered in eking out a subsistence living, the welfare of the entire community is everyone's responsibility:

When sowing time comes, the community meets to discuss how to share out the land — whether each one will have his own plot or if they will work collectively. Everyone joins in the discussion. In my village, for example, we said it was up to all of us if we wanted our own plot or not. But we also decided to keep a common piece of land, shared by the whole community, so that if anyone was ill or injured, they would have food to eat. We worked in that way: each family with their own plot and a large piece of common land for emergencies in the community or in the family. It was mostly to help widows. Each day of the week, someone would go and work that common land.[74]

Menchú's work, and that of her family, will eventually take them beyond their immediate community as they perceive the wider scope of the problem that faces them. The Spanish language is one of the tools Menchú acquires to enable her to move into this broader struggle and to educate and invite others to join her. Reina, from El Salvador, notes the increased empowerment this movement into solidarity with other groups can bring:

This war is not one of just a few, but rather of a whole people. It's a war of the weak against the strong, the pint-sized against the same giants as usual. But the small are not alone. They're united among themselves, and they can count on the support of people from other parts of the world. That gives you confidence, the solidarity we have that we didn't experience before.[75]

Reina mentions the increasing awareness she experiences among, for example, U.S. citizens, regarding the ways in which their government "exploits and bullies the smaller countries."[76] And Onnie Lee Logan remarks that "indeed white people have done black people wrong. And you know what? The general run of em know it."[77] Reina and Onnie are clear about what solidarity means for them. "White people" in the United States, even those of goodwill, have much to do to live into understanding the implications and implementation of authentic solidarity from a position of exploitative privilege.

Past, present, and future dimensions are essential to an adequate understanding of community. Women from communities with a strong sense of their own history frequently synchretize the historical focus of Christianity with their own spiritual traditions. Menchú talks about celebrating all the saints' days that were introduced by Catholicism and says that "ours are not the Saints of the pictures. We celebrate special days talking about our ancestors."[78] Such an understanding enables

Menchú and her people to understand Jesus as a brother still very much alive in the struggles for justice:

> Christ did not die, because generations and generations have followed him. And that's exactly what we understood when our first catechists fell. They're dead but our people keep their memory alive through our struggle against the government, against an enemy who oppresses us.[79]

Menchú rejects secular festivals that celebrate such historical figures as Tecún Umán, because the focus is on something in the past. "For us it would be rejecting him to say that he *was* a hero... because that is talking about him in the past....For us the struggle still goes on today."[80] The "saints" whose memories must be kept alive by the continuing freedom struggles of their people have nothing to do with the painted icons on the walls of white Westerners' churches but are "canonized" in the effect their lives and deaths continue to have. "The *campesinas'* testimonies reveal the cost of peasant struggle and remember those who died, refusing by the retelling to let death be the final word.... Survivors carry history in memory like a hidden wound."[81]

The significance attached to the continuing presence of those who have gone before has much to do with the incredible sense of hope with which communities are sustained to continue working for the ongoing survival of themselves and their children. This commitment to survival has led African-American women, for example, to focus upon "God's response of survival and quality of life to African-American women and mothers of slave descent struggling to sustain their families with God's help," rather than on the "hopelessness of the painful aspects of [their] history."[82]

By their efforts to continue to speak in the voices authentic to their people, and by refusing the imposition of external authorities that must use force to obtain acquiescence, women have continually claimed *strength* in the absence of structural power and have embodied Jesus' words, "I have come that you may have life." Death, violent and bloody, has been the historical experience of many of their communities, yet questions of how to *live* continue to pervade these women's voices and actions. Paula Gunn Allen speaks of the experience of American Indian women:

> Many of the poems written by American Indian women address the stark fact of extinction directly, with a vigor and resilience that does not merely bewail a brutal fate but directs our attention to a kind of hope born of facing the brutal and bitter facts of our recent

history and present condition. This sense of hope is characteristic of the peoples whose history on this continent stretches beyond the dimmest reaches of time, winding back through history to time immemorial; it is a hope that comes about when one has faced ultimate disaster time and time again over the ages and has emerged stronger and more certain of the endurance of the people, the spirits, and the land from which they both arise and which informs both with life.[83]

In the conclusion to her offering of Salvadoran women's stories, Renny Golden observes:

> For women the patriotic action is the act of preserving life, of guaranteeing the people's survival when state terror is unleashed. Dying for the nation is not an objective; survival is. The needs of patriotic honor, or heroism . . . are subsumed to the daily heroism of keeping the community alive. . . .
> The last choice is not who will die, but how to live.[84]

As Allen notes, "The Indians are not doomed to extinction but rather are fated to endure. What a redemptive, empowering realization that is!"[85]

Those struggling for their own and their community's survival, in the process of affirming their own authority and voice, come to a clear recognition of the "sins" that threaten their people and of the grace inherent in movements to reassert their own dignity and right to justice. Such realization is rooted in deep conviction that salvation and the kindom of God are not "pie in the sky" realities awaiting them when they die but are a vision for which they struggle and hope in the midst of the complexities of their contemporary lives. These sins and movements of grace, along with the visions of salvation, are particular to specific times, peoples, and places. Sometimes clear connections can be seen; at other times the relationships are less obvious. The sampling of voices incorporated into this study can do no more than point out the reality of these distinctions and suggest the importance for theological inquiry of engaging such voices in dialogue.

The voices which that spoken in this chapter have done so through the interpretations of translators, scribes, editors, writers, and readers. This mediation must be kept in mind and should induce a healthy suspicion as to the accuracy and adequacy of such portrayals. The degree of mediation necessary to incorporate diverse voices into theo-ethical discourse indicates the degree of *exclusion* still present in academia. Yet the fact that the stories of women such as Onnie Lee Logan, Rigoberta

Menchú, and Amanda are told through the intercession of translators and/or scribes does not render attempts to engage their stories invalid. It *does* demand honesty and humility in terms of the limitations and open-ended nature of any deductions to be made from such engagement. Each woman speaks *from* her own specific location, and not in a way that is necessarily representative of her sisters and brothers, even those who share most closely her own "identity." Each interpreter selects items from any story that she or he finds particularly interesting. Care must be taken not to assume that we have heard all the messages we need to hear from any identifiable community by listening to a few selected voices.

With this caution in mind, I have nevertheless suggested that the diverse expressions and life experiences of the women whose voices provide the primary resources in this chapter do offer some specific challenges to white, Western, masculinist Christianity. As women tell the truths of their lives in the particular modes of expression available to them, they indicate that the "traditional" boundaries between divine and human authority and agency are transgressed. In addition, through reclamation of the validity of their own inner wisdom — motherwit — women assert their convictions that a fuller understanding of truth is possible than that which is captured by the written word alone.

A coalitional theo-ethical enterprise demands the reinterpretation of traditional categories of theological doctrine. In claiming the authority to name and define what constitutes sin and grace, and salvation and the kin-dom of God, in any particular social and historical location, the women who speak here question many of the basic assumptions of what has been promoted as "universal" tenets of Christian faith. The clarity with which these women name their own oppressions and identify the forces that threaten their communities' continuing survival challenges those of us who would be liberation theologians in any sense of that term to take seriously as a theo-ethical resource the multiple expressions of truth that emanate from such diverse contexts.

Chapter 4

Boundaries of Knowledge, Barriers to Knowing
Transforming Epistemologies

How do we know God? How do we know anything? Questions about the nature of coming to knowledge, and of the validation of that knowledge, are fundamental in the development of theo-ethics of voices. The women who have spoken above refuse to see artificially imposed boundaries between ways of knowing and modes of expressing that knowledge as barriers to the exercise of their own authority and agency. Yet such boundaries are still rigidly maintained in much academic discourse, including that which is specifically theo-ethical. Recent feminist explorations in epistemology are helpful in proposing ways in which these boundaries might be seen as distinctions rather than barriers. Similarly, feminist theologians from diverse cultures and locations insist upon the "fiction" of barrier/boundaries between multiple *expressions* of knowledge. These emerging epistemologies provide insight into the methodological development needed for a more fully liberative and participatory theo-ethical enterprise when they are brought into dialogue with the wisdom and knowledge of diverse women's voices.

Wisdom/truth is "spoken" by diverse women through multiple expressions: scientific explorations, art, community activism, sensuality, spirituality, daily tasks, autobiography, and works of myth and imagination. The incorporation of diverse women's voices into feminist/womanist/mujerista projects creates an epistemological rupture in which the white, Western, masculinist modes of knowledge production and validation are seen to be inadequate and exclusionary. Neoplatonic and Aristotelian models of knowing, based as they are on an ideal white, Western, male human, cannot provide space for the "truth" articulated through the voices of Rigoberta Menchú, Onnie Lee Logan, and Suzette Haden Elgin. Biblicist and magisterialist conceptions of Christianity likewise exclude the visions of sin and grace, salvation and the kin-dom, which these women's lives suggest. Feminist, womanist, and mujerista theorists from diverse fields of inquiry are challenging the rigidity of old epistemologies in ways that empower conversation among voices from multiple socio-historical locations.

Diverse ways of knowing do not provide identical "knowledge"; that is why such diversity is critically important in any liberative theo-ethical project. Neither can these multiple modes of knowing be collapsed into a unitary system. But members of many communities sustain hope and agency through their refusal to adopt a rigid compartmentalization between such realities. Ways of coming to knowledge are integrally related to knowledge as a product. To suggest that "knowledge" itself is constructed and thus is *not* a static and quantifiable entity, I substitute the term "knowing" to indicate the dynamic nature of both the process and product of knowledge construction and validation.

Although traditional academic disciplines are only beginning either to validate adequately or to attempt to incorporate multiple voices and perspectives into their formulations of "knowledge," an emphasis on issues of voice and its relationship to knowing has been widespread in feminist theory over the past ten years. Since the publication of Carol Gilligan's *In a Different Voice* in 1982, discussion related to the gender bias of so-called objective approaches to the construction of knowledge has proliferated among feminists.[1] In 1986, Gilligan's text was followed by *Women's Ways of Knowing.*[2] Drawing from many of Gilligan's insights and those of the feminist psychologists and psychiatrists at the Stone Center at Wellesley College,[3] the authors present the results of their interviews with diverse women and propose a framework in which the knowledge patterns of the women interviewed can be categorized. This text is useful for its delineation of certain characteristics that are found in many women's approaches to what they know and how they know it and for its focus on the development of "voice" as women move toward "constructivist knowing."[4]

The first two "ways of knowing" that these authors identify, silence and received knowledge, might better be characterized as psychological states in which oppression has been so internalized that authentic knowing, in the sense of being able to claim some degree of authority and agency, is radically curtailed. Speaking in one's own voice is not perceived as possible in either of these two categories. If "received knowers" begin to recognize the extent to which they "subordinate their own perceptions and judgments to those of others," however, they may make the move into subjectivist knowing, where they will tend initially to trust *only* their own subjectivity.[5] These women do speak in their own voice. Indeed, *only* their own experience is considered trustworthy.

Women who are described as "procedural knowers" come to recognize that their own "gut" can let them down and that a plurality of perspectives is possible, although they still tend either to privilege personal experience or to focus on the development of skills of formal analysis and tools of reason. In procedural knowing, women recognize that their voices need to enter into relationship with the voices of others, although the goal remains one of finding a single unified voice.

Finally, there is the "constructivist knower." I do not share Mary Belenky and her coauthors' reluctance to advocate this position as integrating multiple facets of knowing and thus as most conducive to women's health and agency.[6] As these authors describe them:

> Constructivist women aspire to work that contributes to the empowerment and improvement in the quality of life of others. More than any other group of women in this study, the constructivists feel a part of the effort to address with others the burning issues of the day and to contribute as best they can.... They reveal in the way they speak and live their lives their moral conviction that ideas and values, like children, must be nurtured, cared for, placed in environments that help them grow.[7]

Constructive knowing, as it is here described, reflects the integrated approach to affirming their own knowledge and utilizing it for the empowerment of themselves and their communities that was the goal of the women whose voices were heard above. Onnie Lee Logan, for example, accepted the learning she received at the midwives' classes, but she integrated the new knowledge with her own experience and the learning she had received from her mother and grandmother.[8] Women can come to adopt the characteristics of constructivist knowers through multiple and diverse life experiences that enable them to validate their own authority and agency in the context of their families and communities. A major characteristic of constructivist knowers is this ability to draw in "knowings" from multiple sources.

Belenky and her coauthors conclude by suggesting the need for transformed educational institutions. Although they do not so state it, their goal appears to be educational programs that provide a context in which women may move toward a constructivist approach to knowing. Some of the transformations called for by the authors of *Women's Ways of Knowing* are beginning to emerge in academia. Colleges and universities are instituting more cross-disciplinary courses and programs. Individual teachers and scholars are incorporating works of fiction, poetry, music, and other creative expression into classes other than those specifically devoted to the study of literature or other identifiable art forms. Sometimes this inclusion extends to the forms in which students may express their integration of course material. These trends within feminist epistemologies resonate with the challenges evoked by engaging diverse women's voices and thus add insight and support to the development of a metaphor of voices.

But many of the new insights emerging from these still-embryonic epistemological shifts have yet to find their way into dominating theo-ethical discourse. A friend and colleague was *failed* in a course in her M.Div. program for handing in a creative, artistic, interpretive project instead of the traditional academic paper — to a self-proclaimed "feminist" professor. The student had taken seriously the professor's verbalization of the need for thought and creativity, feeling and emotion, to be more integrated in the academy.

The mere addition of more voices is not sufficient to challenge basic authoritarian structures when rigid boundaries between creativity and action and "legitimate" academic work remain intact.[9] A multiplicity of modes of knowing is not in and of itself the problem. Rather, the difficulty lies in the hierarchical relationship among those expressions, which promotes the validation of some bodies of knowledge and modes of knowing to the exclusion and diminishment of others.[10] The establishment of rigid and hierarchical boundaries, between persons and groups as well as between modes of knowing, is central to the establishment of sovereign authority.[11] Those who would challenge these boundaries must understand both the necessity *and* the consequences of refusing the validity of the authority that holds the barriers in place:

> To disagree with [established] boundaries and definitions, it has been necessary to recognize them; to refuse them is to be shut out even from debate; to transgress them is to mark oneself as mad, heretical, dangerous.... The insights of a mad person, the utterances of a god-possessed saint, the "intuitions" of a woman, the "hunches" of "the common man," the "myths" of non-Western cultures, the "folklore" of lower-caste people, the expressions of women that were written but not "authored" — none of these have been acceptable as expressions or examples of knowledge.[12]

The bounded disciplines described by Elizabeth Minnick, established for various purposes but always serving the function of maintaining particular systems of power, ultimately take on the status of real, essential categories.[13] These categories become so fixed that they are eventually ensconced as the very principles of knowledge itself.[14]

The "transgression" of multiple, artificially imposed boundaries is vitally important. Donna Haraway has used the image of the cyborg to express her insistence that multiple conversations across boundaries apply to our individual existence as well as our lives in relationship with our world and each other.[15] The cyborg is described in the dictionary as "a human being who is linked ... to one or more mechanical devices *upon which some of his* [sic] *vital physiological functions depend.*"[16] Although often associated with the genre of space fiction, the cyborg image might well be applied to the advanced technology often utilized in medical care to maintain the vital functions of a critically ill patient — or to the writer's dependency on her computer. Use of this image does not collapse distinctions between human and machine, but it does, as Haraway points out, illustrate the ambiguous and multifaceted relationships of late twentieth-century humans to their own inventions and constructions, including their constructions of what constitutes knowing:

> By the late twentieth century, our time, a mythic time, we are all chimeras, theorized and fabricated hybrids of machine and organism; in short, we are cyborgs. The cyborg is our ontology; it gives us our politics; The cyborg is a condensed image of both imagination and material reality, the two joined centers structuring any possibility of historical transformation.[17]

The image of the cyborg illuminates the constructed reality both of the external technological world in which we live and also of what constitutes "nature." The boundaries between human and animal, between animal-human organism and machine, and between physical and nonphysical can no longer be held as rigidly defined, if ever they could.[18] Consequently, Haraway describes her work as "an argument for *pleasure* in the confusion of boundaries and for *responsibility* in their construction."[19] Haraway is not eliminating the concept of certain lines of demarcation that distinguish particular components of life and/or thought. Rather, she is insisting that these lines are not and should not be impermeable and that they must be carefully and responsibly articulated.

This responsible confusion of boundaries must be applied to the traditional barriers that exist in the construction and validation of knowing. Patricia Hill Collins writes of the necessity for black women to analyze and challenge the very terms and definitions upon which intellectual discourse is based:

Reclaiming the Black women's intellectual tradition involves examining the everyday ideas of Black women not previously considered intellectuals.... Musicians, vocalists, poets, writers, and other artists constitute another group of Black women intellectuals who have aimed to interpret Black women's experiences.... Producing intellectual work is generally not attributed to Black women artists and political activists.[20]

In her *de*construction of what she perceives as artificial boundaries in the knowledge construction of black women, Collins claims an alternate distinction: that of the difference between "academic" and "intellectual."[21] Such work as that of the music group Sweet Honey in the Rock and playwright Ntozake Shange constitutes serious intellectual work in media that are not traditionally "academic." In reclaiming a black *intellectual* tradition, writers such as Collins, bell hooks, Cornel West, Katie Cannon, and Delores Williams are insisting upon inclusion of those forms of expression that have enabled African-American communities to survive and sometimes even to thrive in the struggles they have faced in racist society. Creative thinkers from a variety of "disciplines" embody the possibility that multiple creative resources are available that challenge the hegemony of bounded knowledges. Because knowing that resides in the embodied reality of knowers, and in creative use of the imagination, is consistently devalued in theo-ethical and other academic discourse, particular attention must be given to the insights such knowing makes possible.

Embodied Knowing: The Practice of Freedom

Feminist and other liberation theorists and practitioners have long disputed the myth of the isolated, objective knower ensconced in "his" ivory tower producing treatises by which to spread the "truth" to an ignorant world.[22] The identification of knowing with distanced and disembodied contemplation, evident in Platonic philosophy and its descendant schools of thought, has had devastating effects on those persons determined by the dominating discourse as being more closely associated with nature and material reality. The association of knowledge with the *nonmaterial* mind and/or soul, increasingly expressed not through passionate voices and action but in words committed to the immortality of print, must be overcome if multiple voices are to bring their critical wisdom and insight to bear on theo-ethical discourse. Many of the women already heard in these pages have refused the authority of this limited conception of knowing. To reiterate the words of midwife Onnie Lee Logan, "I knew what I knew"[23] — and no work is more intricately involved with the task of embodiment than that of a midwife.

In order to examine ways in which the integration embodied by Logan might be enabled in structures still vehemently resistant to challenges to their authority, it is helpful to consider three areas in which the boundaries between action, thought, and feeling have been and are being challenged. First, the feminist claim that the personal is political needs to be examined in both its potential and its liabilities for enhancing liberative praxis. Second, many communities of struggle have developed and articulated a deep understanding of the organic and integrated nature of authentic knowing. Third, liberation theologies, with their emphasis on "praxis," can move the discussion into the explicitly theo-ethical arena.

Feminist Theory: The Personal Is Political

This early catchphrase of a contemporary feminist movement has been useful in bringing to light the political, socially constructed nature of what has been seen historically as women's "personal" lives. Yet emerging as it did from an overly universalized articulation of the split between public and private lives, a dichotomy experienced only by women of economic privilege, the phrase "The personal is political" has been used in such diverse ways as to render it meaningless, and even dangerous, without careful explication of its intended connotations. An individualistic and privatized culture can easily encourage women of privilege to simply assume that their personal experiences and realities can be named "political."[24] An example of the consequences of such a conception is the way in which an all-encompassing obliteration of any distinction between personal and political has led, in some radical lesbian feminist circles, to "one's body and its desires becom[ing] a more reliable guide to one's loyalties than words or public deeds."[25] The gaps and spaces between the personal and political must thus be acknowledged, as well as the connections. This is yet another example of transgressing historically constructed boundaries *and* of maintaining a necessary distinction in the service of liberatory action.

Conscious reflection on personal experience, while important, is not automatically empowering even of the individuals involved. Rigoberta Menchú's autobiography is exemplary in demonstrating the consequences — empowerment *and* great personal risk — of personal reflection that incorporates analysis of socio-historical context and commitment to her community. I have suggested a movement from identity to praxis as a primary criterion for evaluating sources for theo-ethical explorations. This same criterion might be applied to the movement into self-reflection and affirmation that characterizes those white feminist groups who have adopted the "Personal is political" slogan without taking the further steps into social analysis and action. Patricia Hill Collins suggests the importance of the connections between personal experience and consciousness and political action. The goal of the development and sharing of black feminist thought is not individual self-affirmation. Rather, the intent of such theory is to

> infuse Black women's experiences and everyday thought with new meaning by rearticulating the interdependence of Black women's experiences and consciousness. Black feminist thought is *of* African-American women in that it taps the multiple relationships among Black women needed to produce a self-defined Black women's standpoint. *Black feminist thought is for Black women in that it empowers Black women for political activism.*[26]

Personal experience and political activity do not collapse into a single entity. Rather, the two dimensions interact with each other in the context of critical consciousness.

This issue relates to the identification of the stakes of a reader or writer in determining the authority of the text. All acts of reading and writing are "engaged and produced."[27] The concept of "stakes" is not synonymous with the current practice, common in some white feminist work, of outlining one's particularity and using this to excuse critical engagement with material that does not represent one's own essentialized identity. Defining myself as a white, educated woman of relative economic security is no more than a "personal" statement until it is strengthened by a critical assessment of what those characteristics mean when I approach a work by one who does not share them and what action that meaning invokes. Being clear of one's stakes in reading a text involves the politicization of "personal" characteristics by opening up the possibility of engagement in honest dialogue with those who have different stakes.

Communities of struggle do not often have the opportunity to make dramatic distinctions between political and personal issues: what affects any individual cannot be extrapolated from its effect on her or his immediate family and community. For example, the possibility of the "personal" not being involved with the communal politics is not an issue for Menchú.[28] The degree of individualism present in white, Western culture suggests that those with roots in that culture must exercise a particular caution when speaking of the personal as political. Personal conscientization is political to the extent that it empowers individuals into engagement with the structures in which they live their lives and with others who are differently affected by those structures.

Organic Knowing

The authentic incorporation of multiple diverse voices validates the modes of knowing embodied in persons who have not necessarily had access to advanced formal education or any formal education at all. Patricia Hill Collins cites an African-American woman as claiming that she "might not know how to use thirty-four words where three would do, but that does not mean that I don't know what I'm talking about....I know what I'm talking about because I'm talking about myself."[29] This woman suggests that truth resides in concrete acts and feelings directly related to women's own experiences of their lives in the context of their communities.

The knowing that resides in deep feeling is referred to by Hispanic women with the verb *sentir*. Ada María Isasi-Díaz and Yolanda Tarango describe this word as embodying a depth and integration of feeling and knowledge that the English equivalent, "feeling," does not begin to express. When Hispanic women use this term to speak of their relationship with God, it has nothing to do with frivolous, feel-good surface emotions but contains profound faith and knowing:[30]

> Feelings, a human capacity/power of extreme importance in the Hispanic culture, are...intrinsic to the moral criteria of Hispanic Women. The outward expression of feeling is important for the individual Hispanic Woman, and it is also an essential part of her relationship with the community at large. Feelings are indeed "a source of imaginative insight" and a motivation for praxis that goes well beyond any and all reasoning. This is why they have to be understood as intrinsic to principles, to strategies for action — to the struggle for liberation/survival, the way of life of Hispanic Women.[31]

Moral agency and decision-making are thus intricately involved with the depth of knowing that *sentir* expresses in Hispanic women's individual and communal lives.

The experiences described through this term often are not adequately communicated through standard academic prose. Audre Lorde discusses the necessity of poetry to express this consciousness of "living as a situation to be experienced and interacted with," and the ensuing empowerment "more and more to cherish our feelings, and to respect those hidden sources of our power from where true knowledge and, therefore, lasting actions come." In poetry, Lorde finds that she comes closest to expressing this "revelatory distillation of experience....For women, then, poetry is not a luxury."[32] Judy Grahn's poem "The Common Woman" expresses both in form and content the power of poetry to communicate the knowing embedded in the lives of ordinary women:

> the common woman is as common
> as good bread
> as common as when you couldnt go on
> but did.
> For all the world we didnt know we held in common
> all along
> the common woman is as common as the best of bread
> and will rise
> and will become strong—I swear it to you
> I swear it to you on my own head
> I swear it to you on my common
> woman's
> head.[33]

The sharing of experiences through the media of poetry, music, multiple visual art forms, and storytelling, in addition to the prose of autobiography and fiction, is a vital dimension of the knowledge production, validation, and communication of countless communities. This sharing is far more than entertainment, although joy and celebration are frequently present. Describing the telling of life experiences in the context of the oppression and violation of so many of her Asian sisters, Chung Hyun Kyung notes:

> Women's socio-biography brings out the "hidden reality" behind official sociological and historical documents. Listeners of socio-biography hear not cold data but actual people's suffering, crying, and longing. This encounter with foremothers and contemporary sisters in struggle through their storytelling touches Asian women's hearts. It motivates Asian women to participate in the people's struggle for liberation because the people in the stories are real people who tremble with fear and yearn for the touch of their beloved.[34]

Chung has determined that the data for her own theo-ethical work must rise from the socio-biography of her own people. Instead of "the theological puzzles of the people who were the cause of our suffering," the lives of her Korean and other Asian sisters become the "organic" resource from which her own theological questions emerge.[35] The touching of one another's hearts through the authentic sharing and hearing of life stories is the key motivating factor in resistance and the struggle to overcome oppressive systems.

There is a deep sensuality in all of these women's words, in the sense of "passion" described above. This is a passion rooted in *com*passion through its recognition of the intricate relationships between joy and struggle, tears and laughter, pain and the satisfaction gained in keeping on keeping on. Carter Heyward, insisting that this passion is vital to our understandings of ourselves as connected, embodied beings, extends this heart-learning to our nonhuman earth companions:

> I know them all, the people and the trees. I do not know their names, but I know that our sensuality, our shared embodied participation in forming and sustaining the relational matrix that is our home on this planet, is our most common link, and that our sensuality can be trusted.
>
> If we learn to trust our senses, our capacities to touch, taste, smell, hear, see, and thereby know, they can teach us what is good and what is bad, what is real and what is false, for us in relation to one another and to the earth and cosmos.... *Sensuality is a foundation for our authority.*[36]

This is a radical departure from traditional empiricism, despite the commonality of an emphasis on experience. The physical senses do not merely provide data for the mind to absorb as knowledge. Rather, they interact with mind *and emotions* as an integral part of the process of knowing.

Sensuality becomes significant not only in a particular struggle for freedom and self-identification but also as the conduit through which one is able to feel herself connected with liberation struggles with which she has no personal experience. Cherríe Moraga describes her own frustration at being told that her insistence on bringing her own passions into her commitments to her community was divisive:

> I had heard too many times that my concern about specifically sexual issues was divisive to the "larger struggle"... and therefore, not essential for revolution. That to be concerned about the sexuality of women of color was an insult to women in the Third World literally starving to death. But the only hunger I have ever known was the hunger for sex and the hunger for freedom and somehow, in my mind and heart, they were related and certainly not mutually exclusive. If I could not use the source of my hunger as the source of my activism, how then was I to be politically effective?[37]

This awareness of the centrality of individual and communal embodied knowing in the struggle to make connections across lines of both
similarity and difference grounds the theoretical work of women such
as Isasi-Díaz and Tarango, Chung, Heyward, Collins, and Moraga. The
task of "theological technicians" is not to impart theoretical "knowledge" to their communities as much as it is to assist in enabling
these communities to discover the knowledge they already embody,
to generate questions deriving from that knowledge in the social context in which they live their lives, and to locate the resources with
which to continue the process of "constructing" and validating what
they know through the means of storytelling, analysis, liturgizing, and
strategizing.[38]

Liberation Theology and the Hermeneutical Spiral

In his now-classic text, *Pedagogy of the Oppressed,* Paulo Freire notes
that "to speak a true word is to transform the world."[39] Although in
the context of my current project I might paraphrase Freire to read,
"[T]he speech of many *voices* will transform the world," his point is well
taken that the integral relationship of reflection and action, embodied by
the term "praxis," is indeed world-changing. Liberation theologians in
many parts of the world have drawn upon Freire's pedagogical insights
in developing understandings of the praxis of their own communities. One study where the key elements of this praxis are particularly
clearly laid out is that of Ada María Isasi-Díaz and Yolanda Tarango as
they outline the liberation method that emerges from Hispanic women's
historical experiences.

Although they distinguish four movements in the process, the authors
insist that "these four movements are interwoven and interfacing....
Most of the time one is not understood if all are not understood."[40]
Isasi-Díaz and Tarango identify these components as "sharing our stories," analysis, liturgizing, and strategy. In the sharing of stories, women
"claim the events of their lives, along with themselves as persons, [as]
important and relevant" and come to greater confidence in their abilities to know and to act. They realize that their perceptions are shared
by other members of their communities and can affirm that divine
revelation is indeed present in their own personal and communal lives.[41]

Analysis is a difficult and complex dimension of the spiral, yet it is
crucial in the development of critical consciousness. Even "enablers"
who are from the community are often tempted to conclude that their
people are not ready or able to understand the complexity of their situation. In the experience of Isasi-Díaz and Tarango, however, "[T]he

group is always willing and capable if the analysis is based on the lived experience of the members of the group."[42]

In the naming of "liturgizing" as a component of their praxis spiral, Isasi-Díaz and Tarango depart in a significant dimension from the system initiated by Freire and developed further by Joe Holland and Peter Henriot.[43] Holland and Henriot name this facet of their model "theological reflection." Isasi-Díaz and Tarango's use of the term "liturgizing" invites movement beyond the rather limited academic activity suggested by the word "theological" and invokes a "natural and spontaneous way of relating to the divine," a way that incorporates the "high value [placed] on feelings and emotions" without denying the presence of reason and that acknowledges and values the participation of all in the community.[44]

Finally, Isasi-Díaz and Tarango turn to strategizing. Without movement into action, the other facets of the praxis spiral break down into a merely circular process that does not further progress toward liberation. The people themselves design their own strategies to transform unjust relationships of power, disclosed in the preceding storytelling and analysis, for "only the community involved knows the risks it is willing to take."[45]

At every point on this dynamic and open-ended spiral, all four components are present and interacting in some way, and the contributions of all members of the community are valued. By holding these elements together, and by refusing to give credibility to proposals that privilege any one over and to the exclusion of the others, Isasi-Díaz and Tarango, along with diverse liberation practitioners, define "praxis." There are clearly moments in time when one dimension will be temporarily more in focus than the others and/or more critical for a particular community in a particular situation. Yet the integrated theological praxis that emerges from Hispanic women's commitments to their communities cannot be rigidly compartmentalized. The integral relationship of the diverse elements of liberation praxis has yet to inform adequately academic theology *or* other "theoretical" disciplines. Isasi-Díaz and Tarango insist:

> To *do* theology is to free theology from the exclusive hold of academia; it is also a matter of denouncing the false dichotomy between thought and action so prevalent in Western culture. To do theology is to recognize that the source of theology is human existence, its questions and concerns as well as its beliefs. To do theology is to validate and uphold the lived experience of the oppressed, since the dominant cultures and countries not only deny its validity, but even question its very existence.[46]

Hispanic women do not look to the official church to validate their praxis. "Whether these religious understandings and beliefs are sanctioned by the 'proper' church authorities is irrelevant to [them]."[47] Praxis is evaluated in terms of the extent to which it empowers the continuing struggle for justice for individuals and for their communities.

An embodied approach to knowing insists upon recognition of the multiple modes of construction, validation, and expression of that which constitutes knowledge/truth/wisdom. Such an approach, long affirmed by many communities that have been excluded from the so-called traditional avenues of knowledge production, allows for the incorporation of multiple voices and perspectives into theo-ethical discourse. The challenge of embodied knowing, with its transgression of the boundaries of thought and feeling, body and mind/spirit, reflection and action, demands similar transgression of some of the boundaries between the more "traditional" conceptions of knowledge.

Creative Knowing: The Genre of Theo-ethical Discourse

An embodied approach to the revelation of the sacred in the world acknowledges that "God" speaks throughout creation and particularly in the interactions and relationships of human and other-than-human created beings. I do not engage the science/creationism debate here, and I am not concerned primarily with the boundaries still held in some fields of discourse between the sciences and religion. Rather, I *assume* the cocreative dimensions of both the sciences and theo-ethical explorations and turn my attention instead to the question of imaginative knowing, which is often marginalized in both arenas.

Imagination and creativity are deeply embedded in the religious impulses of all cultures. One has only to look at the work of the "great masters" of Western culture to discern the overwhelming presence of religious themes, whether in painting, sculpture, music, fiction, or poetry. Museums around the world are being challenged to return "art works" from indigenous cultures to their rightful owners, for whom they have profoundly religious significance. A piece of sculpture named *Christa* can invoke intense and conflictual theological debate because of the power of symbol and creativity.

A spirit of imaginative inquiry and faith underlies both theo-ethical and scientific investigations. The boundaries between imagination and truth, creativity and scientific objectivity, art and the so-called hard knowledges, are permeable indeed. Both "science" and "theology-ethics" are about the tasks of meaning-making. Philosopher Mary

Midgley discusses imagination as a vital process linking scientific and religious endeavors:

> [Good scientists] tend to have a very strong guiding imaginative system. Their world-picture is usually a positive and distinctive one, with its own special drama. They do not scrupulously avoid conveying any sense of dark and light, of what matters and what does not, of what is to be aimed at and what avoided at all costs.[48]

The sense of faith, or "choice about how to regard the universe," is not a problem to be avoided or eliminated. Rather, it is to be acknowledged and "rightly directed."[49] Indeed, Midgley says,

> Scientists, merely by being scientists, can find themselves using and resting in an attitude which is in a plain sense religious. The intellectual attitude necessary for science, if given its full scope and not reduced artificially to a mere mindless tic for collecting, is continuous with a typically religious view of the physical world. This is one of the varieties of religious experience.[50]

The imaginative enterprise of seeking to "understand and contemplate the world" is at the heart of both scientific and religious endeavors. This creative impulse is behind all major scientific discoveries, as well as behind the most lasting insights of religious thinkers. According to Midgley, it is not merely difficult to keep this impulse out of our more factual exploration, "It is conceptually impossible."[51]

This link between imaginative and factual knowing, central to both scientific and religious epistemological systems, suggests, as noted above, that science *fiction* may also be considered a significant source for explorations in both fields of endeavor. The imaginative literature included in this genre offers transformative possibilities for rethinking the boundaries between modes of knowing and their expressions, as well as the relationships among knowers and between knowers and their human and other-than-human contexts.

"Science fiction" — as well as other creative speculative literature — has the power to transcend the supposed limits of the earthbound human and the ways of knowing that have long been entrenched in Western academic traditions, not through an "escape" from bodiliness or responsibility but by splitting open the barriers to creative possibility. A friend recently shared with me her experience of "coming out" as a lesbian to her fifteen-year-old brother. He received her news with unexpected calm and an acceptance that went beyond mere tolerance. When my friend asked how he had managed to achieve such an attitude, her brother replied, "I guess because I read so much science fiction."[52] The diverse literature included in this genre offers to white, relatively privileged readers accessibility into considerations of difference and domination in ways less fraught with the danger of co-optation than does, for example, the work of African-American women novelists. This is not to imply that these latter works, as well as critical engagement with *persons* from diverse locations, are not crucial in any liberating theo-ethic. Yet the capacity to envision possible futures that break free of the constraints of the "real" world, and to imagine and grapple with some of the new dilemmas that might emerge there, is also an inherently theo-ethical enterprise. Speculative fiction offers one additional creative point of entry into the process of justice-making.

The term "science fiction" frequently conjures up images of *Star Wars*-type novels and movies in which futuristic technologies are employed in the furtherance of the contemporary political project of world domination by the self-proclaimed "good guys" (that is, the United States — us), whose role is to protect "democracy" around the world. A broader understanding is suggested by use of the abbreviation SF.[53] The radical shift in understanding that this signifier makes possible is exemplified by the inclusion of "scientific fact" — under which such scientists as Donna Haraway include their own explorations.[54] In addition, Marleen Barr adds "space fiction," claiming that "feminist fabulation enables readers to pioneer *spaces* beyond patriarchal boundaries."[55] As well as creating a space in which nonpatriarchal worlds and worldviews can be imagined, "[F]eminist SF metaphorically facilitates an understanding of sexism as a story authored by men who use their power to make women the protagonists of patriarchal fictions."[56]

The importance of the insights of Haraway and Barr is that their use of SF, both as signifier and resource, exposes the reality that many of the "facts" that we are expected to accept as given in particular fields of discourse are indeed fictional constructions of the patriarchal imagination. Important in this discussion is the relationship of facts, fiction, and truth. "Facts are opposed to opinion, to prejudice, but not to fiction. Both fiction and fact are rooted in an epistemology that appeals to experience," maintains Haraway, pointing to the active quality of fiction as "a present act of fashioning," whereas "fact is a descendant of a past participle, a word form which masks the generative deed or performance. A fact seems done, unchangeable."[57]

The adverse reaction of many Christians when the Bible is described as "myth" is testimony to the disassociation of so-called truth from the wisdom that is embedded in powerful narratives that do not depend on unassailable historical facticity for their relevance and wisdom. SF writer Ursula Le Guin is adamant about the truth in fantasy:

Fantasy is true, of course. It isn't factual, but it is true. Children know that. Adults know it too and that is precisely why many of them are afraid of fantasy. They know that its truth challenges, even threatens, all that is false, all that is phony, unnecessary, and trivial in the life they have let themselves be forced into living. They are afraid of dragons, because they are afraid of freedom.[58]

The "way of art" is precisely *not* either to shut out the senses and emotions *or* to "blind the mind's eye." Rather, art's task, whether it be painting, music, poetry, or SF, is "to keep open the tenuous difficult, essential connections between the two extremes. To connect. To connect the idea with value, sensation with intuition, cortex with cerebellum."[59] SF is a descriptive term that can help us to understand our current reality in metaphorical and imaginative terms that have the power to break through the constrictive vision a fearful world imposes on our senses:

> Science fiction properly conceived, like all serious fiction, however funny, is a way of trying to describe what is in fact going on, what people actually do and feel, how people relate to everything else in this vast sack, this belly of the universe, this womb of things to be and tomb of things that were, this unending story. In it, as in all fiction, there is room enough to keep even Man where he belongs, in his place in the scheme of things.[60]

The theo-ethical task of finding new metaphors and images through which to envision and act upon transformed relationships among humans and between humans and all other dimensions of the universe is enriched through the genre of SF.

Despite the apparent relevance of SF literature for constructive theo-ethical work, the genre is seldom used as a resource for such projects. Sallie McFague is one feminist theologian who has suggested the depth of this relevance and claimed a place for speculative fiction as a theological resource in her assertion that "one of the most powerful ways to question a tradition is to imagine new worlds that challenge it."[61] The "new worlds" imagined in transformative feminist SF are not unlike references to the "kingdom" in Christian tradition, except that they are imaged through the life experiences of women.

SF writer and scripture scholar Marti Steussy insists that "my fiction, my scholarship, and my teaching flow from the same well. To tell you about my fiction is to tell you also about my theology and spirituality." Steussy describes her delight in the aliens she creates for her fiction and notes how they challenge her assumptions about humanity:

What would happen if we — western society in general, Christianity in particular... — really faced the insights of contemporary physics, astronomy, mathematics, chemistry, biology, and the social sciences? What if we really thought about our smallness in the bigness of space? What if we looked at the continuum which connects us, physically and psychologically, to the animal world? *Fundamentalists warn that such ideas change religion. I agree. I do not agree that we should flee the change.*[62]

This change is the very stuff of theology and involves seeing God as continually involved in creation through evolution of our own and other species. This being the case, the evolution/creationism debate is moot, and we are challenged to reexamine the false dichotomies we create between the natural or scientific and the theological.[63]

Steussy is aware that SF is written predominantly by a morally engaged community that has experienced organized religion as "superstitious, intolerant and authoritarian."[64] Those who are convinced that mere adjustment of old theological systems will not serve to respond to contemporary issues cannot afford to ignore the ways in which SF can enable us to "reconsider the very categories of the God-transcends-humanity as man-transcends-woman as humanity-transcends-nature worldview."[65]

The work of such writers as Le Guin, Steussy, Octavia Butler, Margaret Atwood, and Suzette Haden Elgin offers a neglected but rich source for theo-ethical wisdom. Far from being escapist, as many of its critics charge, SF, as conceived by authors such as Le Guin, Haraway, and Barr, has the potential to open a doorway onto worlds more "real" than those most of us inhabit. Indeed, given the extent of our immersion in current patterns of knowing and of what constitutes trustworthy truth, "realistic" texts may be able to mirror only the patriarchal "reality" that pervades contemporary existence.[66] bell hooks may be noting a similar difficulty when she suggests that black women's fiction "breaks new ground in that it clearly names the ways structures of domination, racism, sexism, and class exploitation, oppress,... yet these writings often fail to depict any location for the construction of new identities."[67] The feminist utopias sometimes offered in SF offer "postmodern challenges to patriarchal master narratives."[68]

The contemporary Western mind-set still labors often under the illusion that with adequate research effort, and perhaps enough studies and books, we will eventually get it right and solve the problems facing us in the contemporary world. The proliferation of "problem books" addressing issues of drugs, divorce, racism, pregnancy of unmarried women, co-dependency, loneliness, and so forth exemplifies this attitude in a popularized form. To Ursula Le Guin,

> That is escapism, that posing evil as a "problem," instead of what it is: all the pain and suffering and waste and loss and injustice we will meet all our lives long, and must face and cope with over and over and over, and admit, and live with, in order to live human lives at all.[69]

Seeking to move out of oppressive, mind-constricting situations through the medium of SF or other creative modes of expression is not "escapist" to Le Guin, any more than were the attempts of "the captured soldier tunneling out of prison, the runaway slave, and Solzenhitsyn in exile."[70] In liberatory SF, speculative fiction that is authentically grounded in the movement toward freedom,

> All the doors stand open, from the prehuman past through the incredible present to the terrible and hopeful future. All connections are possible. All alternatives are thinkable. It is not a comfortable, reassuring place. It's a very large house, a very drafty house. But it's the house we live in.
>
> And science fiction seems to be the modern literary art which is capable of living in that huge and drafty house, and feeling at home there, and playing games up and down the stairs, from basement to attic.[71]

All good art *and* science must move beyond descriptions of "how" things are and ask "Why?" before moving back to asking, "How can they be different?" In this way, science becomes more than mere technology, and art more than "trivial entertainment." In both cases, the possibility is offered for movement to "intelligent ethical choice,"[72] in fact, for movement into a "constructivist knowing" with profound relevance for theo-ethical discourse.

The weaving together of SF narratives, in all their multiple meanings, offers a possibility for creative and integrated approaches to knowing that acknowledge the constructed nature of what we perceive as truth, regardless of claims to divine revelation beyond human mediation. Donna Haraway once again embraces the power of the stories that result from such integration:

> There is an aesthetic and an ethic built into thinking of scientific practice as storytelling, an aesthetic and ethic different from capitulation to "progress" and belief in knowledge as passive reflection of "the way things are," and also different from the ironic skepticism and fascination with power so common in the social studies

of science. The aesthetic and ethic latent in the examination of storytelling might be pleasure and responsibility in the weaving of tales. Stories are means to ways of living. Stories are technologies for primate embodiment.[73]

Story and myth are central in the Christian and most, if not all, other religious traditions. When the stories of SF are brought into dialogue with narrative and other creative voices from multiple contexts and locations, our "ways of living" may indeed be transformed by the resulting conversations and action.

Valorizing the many ways in which multiply situated knowers share their stories and embody diverse modes and expressions of knowing is critical for the development of a theo-ethics of voices. Women from diverse communities, and from diverse locations within those communities, raise questions and struggle toward better quality of life for themselves and their people. Feminist/womanist/mujerista "liberation" theologians, with their understandings of praxis as incorporating reflection and action into an integrated process, offer glimpses of the possibilities of welcoming multiple expressions and articulations of knowing in theo-ethical discourse. The works of Rigoberta Menchú and Onnie Lee Logan suggest the mutually enhancing relationship between theory-making and activism. Their contributions to both method and content are at least as valuable to the theo-ethical life of their communities as are the insights of their academically trained sisters and brothers.

The creativity of those who develop and utilize their own modes of knowing for the survival of their people is evident in the defense strategies developed by Menchú and her people[74] and in the ingenuity of some homeless women who develop their own "entrepreneurship" for economic survival.[75] Creativity and imagination are prototypically present in the genre of SF. This body of literature provides another medium for new visions of alternative social structures and has the potential to participate in the shattering of barriers created by the "fictions" of racism, sexism, heterosexism, and economic exploitation. That SF that focuses explicitly on relationships with "aliens" suggests new possibilities for looking at our interactions with those who are different from ourselves in significant dimensions of our socio-historical location.[76] Other SF involves enhancing human talents to offer alternatives to contemporary problems: this form includes not only the cyborg but also persons with psi (psychic abilities) talents.[77] The fact that many SF works are coauthored, and that worlds created by one author are frequently later taken up and further developed by others, implies the possibility of coalition and solidarity even in the development of printed text.[78]

The importance of maintaining a vision is attested to by diverse communities of women. Isasi-Díaz and Tarango quote one of their interviewees as stating that "the most important thing in the life of any person [is] to have a vision. Because, even if everything goes wrong, if you have a vision, you will continue *luchando* [struggling] because that vision is something stronger than you."[79] Chung Hyun Kyung insists on the importance of this vision for Asian women when she asserts that "Asian women know they cannot endure meaningless suffering if they do not dream of a world defined by wholeness, justice, and peace."[80] "If critical reflection enables them to see the oppressive power of the false self imposed upon them by patriarchal society, women's creativity enables them to discover their true self."[81] Echoing the words of Le Guin, Chung describes theology for Asian women as "a language of hope dreams and poetry" that is "not a luxury.... Theology as vision quest is not an escapist, otherworldly addiction of the oppressed."[82] bell hooks speaks of "all the time black folks (especially the underclass) spend just fantasizing about what our lives would be like if there were no racism, no white supremacy."[83] This vision and creativity will have infinitely varied forms of expression within and among different communities of struggle. They are a central source of the articulation of theologies from those communities; they must become a central challenge to re-form masculinist theology into an authentic plurality of theologies of voice.

Diverse ways of knowing must be incorporated into the definitions of how and what we know. Logan knows what she knows, and the licensing procedure of the state is irrelevant. God has given her a gift, and she will use it. Varied approaches to knowledge must be understood as related to each other rather than existing within clearly defined boundaries. Varied modes of knowing are kept alive often by the efforts of those whose voices have been seldom heard and still more rarely heeded in the formulation of both secular and religious canons. Yet asserting the significance of such inclusion is clearly inadequate. I now turn to the problematic relationships that have existed historically among those engaged in diverse forms of knowledge production. I suggest that, in facing some of the challenges of the struggle to recognize and overcome the unequal power dynamics currently pervading notions of "difference," we might be able finally to recognize our differences as empowering resources in our theo-ethical praxis.

Chapter 5

Boundaries of Identity, Barriers to Voices
Transforming Our Praxis

The task of moving into authentic dialogue — engaging multiple voices in conversation — across the differences that historically have divided and alienated person from person, human from other animal, material from "spirit" is both immensely difficult and critically important if we are to do more than merely talk about justice. Recognizing and affirming differences among ourselves and in our ways of knowing are necessary starting points, but without the socio-political analysis that demystifies the power imbalances inherent in many of those differences, movement into greater freedom and authenticity is paralyzed. African-American, Latina, Asian-American, lesbian, and other women whose voices have not been central in the formulation of white feminist theory take the risk of once again being diminished or violated by moving into dialogue. White women are anxious about being exposed as "racist," and often are fearful of the rage they may encounter, anger that is not easier to deal with because it is understandable. They may come to discussion almost paralyzed by such tensions. But the systems against which we all must struggle are very much intact and feed voraciously off any dimensions of our lives that keep us apart from one another. The question cannot be *whether* to attempt to bring our voices into critical engagement with each other; it must be *how*.

Any discussion of a praxis that involves diverse groups must attend to the issue of identity. Communities struggling to overcome situations of exploitation and domination deal constantly with both subtle and explicit insistence that something is *essentially* disordered in their very personhood. Living in the context of a dominating social reality that is in direct conflict with their own best interests, oppressed peoples have devised strategies of resistance to affirm their own self-worth and to refute the definitions imposed upon them from outside of their own communities. This resistance has made use of, and in many ways has made possible, the multiple modes of knowledge construction and validation discussed above. Thus any attempt to dialogue with the voices emerging from such communities must take into account the significance of group identity in the production and valorization of knowledge.

In the contemporary context of diverse and interlocking struggles for justice, however, an overemphasis on group identity sometimes has contributed to polarization and even hostility between and within communities of exploited peoples. No one individual has a single, unitary "identity." Effective political action is enhanced when assumptions of an essentialist conception of "woman," "black," "poor," "lesbian," and so forth are replaced by images of "cyborg" individuals and communities that acknowledge their inherent multiplicity and diversity. I have challenged the acceptance of rigid boundaries between diverse ways of knowing, suggesting that recognition and affirmation of certain distinctions do not necessitate hierarchically defined and hegemonically enforced lines of demarcation. I now suggest that a similar approach to racial, sexual, economic, and other identities might enable movement toward an authentic solidarity in struggle and ultimately empower the development of theologies of voices.

All communities of struggle, and all individuals within those communities, need spaces that provide nurturance and self-validation. Yet such spaces must not replicate the dominant culture's exclusionary practices in terms of rigid definitions of who does or does not "belong." The importance of community in establishing a sense of identity and empowering struggles for survival/liberation must not be underestimated; on the other hand, it is necessary to examine some of the tensions that arise within communities over the issue of identity.

Community and Identity

For the minority of men who fit and accept the dominant cultural norm — young, white, virile, affluent, English-speaking, heterosexual — the images of advertising, television shows, and political, religious, educational, and social institutions of power reinforce a positive sense of identity.[1] I am concerned here with those who do *not* see their own image reflected to any great extent by these media. The need for a community base through which to gain a sense of self in opposition to dominant cultural stereotypes is evidenced in the extent to which women *and* men internalize and adopt as "ideal" the images reflected to them in the mirror of the culture in which they must (or choose to) live. That some construction of community be developed to provide such affirmation is vital; the *form* that such community might take is less easily articulated.

Community Identity and the Struggle for Survival

The concept of community has been much struggled over and written about in recent years. The individualized nature of white, Western, masculinist culture, continuing unabated in economic, political, educational, and ecclesial institutions as well as in individual lives, leaves many feeling isolated, lonely, and in despair. The success of M. Scott Peck's book *The Different Drum* is testimony to the extent to which groups as diverse as parish congregations and business executives have turned to techniques of "community-building" to enhance everything from personal well-being to worker productivity to peace and disarmament.[2] I do not deny that there are some strategies that can enhance any group's ability to work and live together, to form "community." However, I selected the word "and" in the heading for this section deliberately. Authentic community, that which genuinely empowers its members both in terms of their self-esteem *and* in their efforts to improve the quality of life for themselves and their sisters and brothers, is forged in the relationship between struggle and community. The nature of the struggle and the form of the resulting community are in direct relationship: struggles that focus on the achievement of human dignity and justice for all enhance the growth of communities that can accommodate and appreciate differences in their socio-political and other institutions.[3]

The Centrality of Community: The writers of theological and other texts emerging from diverse liberation contexts are clear that a major distinction between their work and that of their white, male, Western forebears is their *recognition* of their rootedness in and accountability with their communities of origin.[4] This "community" not only consists of the current members of the group but is also radically inclusive of those who have gone before and deeply concerned for those who will come after. A Salvadoran friend shares with me her experience of returning to her homeland for the Day of the Dead, when families gather in the cemetery for festive picnics at the graves of loved ones. The music group Sweet Honey in the Rock sings that "those who have died have never left..../ [T]he dead have a pact with the living."[5] The *Presente!*

proclaimed in litanies naming the martyred in Central America invokes both the ongoing participation of those who have died and the commitment of the living to continue the struggle. Cherríe Moraga speaks of her mother "remembering in her blood" the past debasement of her family and community,[6] while Audre Lorde appeals to such "blood memory" to challenge her African-American sisters to greater support of one another:

> We are African women and we know, in our blood's telling, the tenderness with which our foremothers held each other. It is that connection which we are seeking. We have the stories of black women who healed each other's wounds, raised each other's children, fought each other's battles, tilled each other's earth, and eased each other's passages into life and into death. We know the possibilities of support and connection for which we all yearn, and about which we dream so often.[7]

The connections articulated by these women are more powerful than the mere sterile knowledge that if certain liberative possibilities happened once, they may be possible again. Moraga, Lorde, and their sisters know themselves to be deeply related both to the liberating and oppressive realities of their past and to those who struggled to survive within such contexts. Relationships with one's foremothers empower action in the present, for the future.

If access to such a past is important, so too is maintaining the collective memory of the community in ways that continue to empower today's members. bell hooks speaks of this community as "homeplace":

> Throughout our history, African-Americans have recognized the subversive value of homeplace, of having access to private space where we do not directly encounter white racist aggression. Whatever the shape and direction of black liberation struggle,... domestic space has been a crucial site for organizing, for forming political solidarity. Homeplace has been a site of resistance. Its structure was defined less by whether or not black women and men were conforming to sexist behavior norms and more by our struggle to uplift ourselves as a people, our struggle to resist racist domination and oppression.[8]

Such space, for hooks, is not to be confused with separatist or even Black Nationalist movements. Rather, it is akin to what Alice Walker suggests when she speaks of a womanist as "not a separatist, except periodically for health."[9] The dimension of health is a matter of survival.

While acknowledging the significance of working in coalition with diverse people, Bernice Johnson Reagon still insists that "you better be sure you got your home someplace for you to go to so that you will not become a martyr to the coalition. Coalition *can* kill people."[10]

The critical need for community must be addressed within the context of pressures to assimilate into the dominating culture. As a Jewish woman, Melanie Kaye/Kantrowitz is aware that "assimilation is a much larger issue than who you do or don't look like." Historically, "Jewish people have vacillated between forced identification and forced assimilation."[11] A sense of one's own history and culture is immensely valuable — and deeply vulnerable — in a society committed to the erasure and/or subordination of difference.

Community and Liberation Struggle: Salvadoran Archbishop Oscar Romero's pronouncement that, should he be killed, he would live on in the struggle of his people emphasizes the power of a deep sense of communal identity. Personal security that betrays the long-term survival of the people is unthinkable. And although concerns for one's own community remain foremost, efforts to achieve personal self-identity and autonomy must be undertaken in a context that "does not manipulate nor diminish any other person or community." On the contrary,

> Hispanic Women achieve survival/liberation when they risk, when they struggle, when they love, when they use their creative power for the good of the community.... The struggle for liberation has to do not only with commitment by a given Hispanic Woman, but also with her relations with others within her community and with other communities that also struggle for liberation.[12]

Clearly, a distinction is being made here between other communities that struggle, and with whom one must stand in solidarity, and the so-called communities of the oppressor. Yet "the good" is clearly identified with using one's gifts for the growth and enhancement of the community. Evil is failure to do so.

For African-American communities, the black church has been one institution over which control has been maintained by the community itself, from the "invisible institution" of the days of enslavement to the churches in African-American communities today. Katie Cannon notes how "the faith assertions of the Black Church encouraged slaves to reject any teachings that attempted to reconcile slavery with the gospel of Jesus Christ." Far from being passively accepted as the "opium" of the oppressors, "[S]lave religion was dominated by a tradition of defiance which emphasized the communal struggle for survival."[13] In a time when familial ties were *not* under the control of enslaved peoples, and children and other family members could be sold away at any time without notice, communal relationships that were not defined by blood ties were of critical significance.

"Homeplace" for such peoples has little to do with the hunger for safe and nurturing places where one can remain safe and unchallenged by the realities of the wider world and its tensions, although those involved day by day in struggles for their very lives do indeed need moments of such space. Neither is the sense of self that comes from the struggle the motivating factor. Sustenance comes from actual engagement in communities of resistance and, according to bell hooks and Cornel West, can be found only in such a location.[14] hooks and West suggest that the current resurgence of Black Nationalism reflects feelings of having lost a true sense of community. While concerned that the neonationalist movement tends to be dehistoricized and lacking in adequate social and cultural analysis, these authors acknowledge this development as symptomatic of the need for the preservation of hope that is possible only within the context of communities of resistance.[15] The fact that contemporary racism is less easily identified in its structures than was the case during slavery means that new means must be found both to articulate the problems facing African-Americans in the late twentieth century and to form a basis for communal resistance struggle:

> The "chitlin-circuit" — that network of black folks who knew and aided one another — has been long broken.... We cannot return to the past. While it is true that we lost closeness, it was informed by the very structure of racist domination black civil rights struggle sought to change....
>
> The identity crisis we suffer has to do with losing a sense of political perspective, not knowing how we should struggle collectively to fight racism and to create a liberatory space to construct radical black subjectivity. *This identity has to do with resistance, with reconstructing a collective front to re-vision and renew black liberation struggle.*[16]

The critical necessity for "collective organized struggle," rather than a focus merely on African-American identity, informs hooks's call for community and "homeplace."[17]

The collective struggle of the people includes multiple strategies and talents, including those of academic theorists who see their own work as intrinsically related to the resistance struggles of their people. Education is not seen as a personal gift or achievement. Rather, Katie Cannon suggests, "[T]he Black female was taught that her education was meant not to 'uplift' her alone but also to prepare her for a life of service in the 'uplifting' of the Black community."[18] Likewise, Ada María Isasi-Díaz and Yolanda Tarango speak of themselves as "theological technicians," with particular gifts that are to be used in the service of the community but that are not more important than the gifts that others have to share.[19]

What distinguishes these women from their white, Western, masculinist theological "colleagues" is their *recognition* of the nonindividualized basis of their knowledge and accountability. The pages that have poured forth over the centuries from ecclesial and academic ivory towers also have their roots in the social structures and locations from which their authors emerged. These tomes have played a major role in maintaining those structures, ideologies, and misapprehensions. Recognition of the connection between knowledge production and the particular societal/communal context from which authors of such knowledge come is of critical importance in any effort to resist hegemonic sources of ideology and exploitation and to envision new possibilities for the future.

Community, Identity, and Exclusion

Recognition of the vital importance of a strong sense of identity based on racial, cultural, sexual, or other "identity" does not imply that such identities are unproblematic. To the contrary, issues of identity and community are deeply complex. Some of the ambiguous dimensions of both community and identity are experienced by persons who find themselves less than adequately embodied in any one specific community or "homeplace." When some part of one's identity does not "fit" within the definition put forward by the majority of those constituting the group, any tendency toward reducing identity to a fixed essence is thrown into sharp relief.

Problems of Belonging: From the days of Sojourner Truth's "Aint I a Woman?" speech, questions of definition have arisen within feminist movements. Challenging white women who defined womanhood in terms of their own protected and privileged experience, Truth insisted on claiming for herself a definition that included her own very different reality. By both hidden and overt assumptions of normativity, white European and Euro-American feminists continue to replicate the very hegemonic structures they seek to transform. It is increasingly clear that there is no such thing as "woman's experience," but only women's experiences, multiple and constructed through myriad factors of social and cultural location. In theological circles, one can no longer speak of "theology" in the singular, given the diverse expressions that emerge from a multiplicity of liberation communities.

But it is not only the category of "woman" that has been challenged as inadequate for the incorporation of a plurality of experiences. Women within diverse communities are insisting that the multiple identities that they frequently embody must be welcomed into the definition of who "belongs." Audre Lorde speaks of her own struggle to have her lesbian identity accepted and acknowledged as a vital part of who she was and as central to her political commitments in diverse contexts: "Any world which did not have a place for me loving women was not a world in which I wanted to live, not one which I could fight for."[20] Lorde continues:

> *Being women together was not enough. We were different. Being gay-girls together was not enough. We were different. Being Black together was not enough. We were different. Being Black women together was not enough. We were different. Being Black dykes together was not enough. We were different.*
>
> Each of us had our own needs and pursuits, and many different alliances. Self-preservation warned some of us that we could not afford to settle for one easy definition, one narrow individuation of self.... At the Bag, at Hunter College, uptown in Harlem, at the library, there was a piece of the real me bound in each place, and growing.[21]

It is a common experience for women to find themselves in contexts, often those very locations where they had thought to find themselves "at home," and discover that some part of them is not welcome, must be kept quiet, is considered dangerous to the unity of the group. But, says Lorde, "Only when I integrate all the parts of who I am, openly,...can I bring myself and my energies as a whole to the service of those struggles which I embrace as part of my living."[22]

Lesbian women from many communities have experienced the dynamic about which Lorde speaks. When the battered women's movement began to challenge the *structures* that inhibited women's capacity to act on their own behalf to free themselves from their batterers, it found itself a target of "lesbian baiting," which resulted in withdrawal by many funding sources. Lesbian women, who had been at the heart of the movement, were asked to leave or at least to keep their identity closeted, "in the best interests of the movement."[23] Cherríe Moraga relates a similar experience within her own community:

A political commitment to women must involve, by definition, a political commitment to lesbians as well. To refuse to allow the Chicana lesbian the right to the free expression of her own sexuality, and her politicization of it, is in the deepest sense to deny one's self the right to the same.... There will be no change among heterosexual men ... as long as the Chicano community keeps us lesbians and gay men political prisoners among our own people. Any movement built on the fear and loathing of anyone is a failed movement.[24]

Explicit in Moraga's analysis is the loss that ensues to the whole community when particular voices are silenced.

Of course, lesbian women are not immune from similar expressions of exclusion. The claim is sometimes put forward by radical lesbian separatists that "the only 'women-only' there are are lesbian women." Speaking at the Michigan Women's Music Festival, Bernice Johnson Reagon challenged this idea, insisting that such claims "give me a big problem, cause I would have to leave too many of my folk out.... *And if they came in they would be homophobic.* And you'll have to challenge them about it. Can you handle it?"[25] It is as impossible to grow up in the current social and political climate in the United States without absorbing unhealthy doses of homophobia as it is to grow up without absorbing racist stereotypes and attitudes. More and more, women from diverse and multiple locations are insisting, with Lorde, Moraga, and Reagon, that we are indeed in a situation of having to grapple with such realities together or to retreat to our little "barred rooms," with the result that "when those who call the shots get ready to clean house, they have easy access to [us]."[26] Clichés like "divide and conquer" would not have endured without some basis in reality.

Obviously, lesbian identity is not the only facet of women's lives that can be unacceptable within particular "community" contexts. Caryatis Cardea speaks of her sense of exclusion as a working-class woman in many lesbian feminist contexts, where she experiences much of what is named as "feminist process" as middle-class white women's dependence on a therapy model.[27] Central to Cardea's argument is the sometimes subtle demand that women speak to one another in a particular manner — that voices that differ, particularly in pitch and volume, are written off as unworthy of a hearing. There are many challenges yet to be faced in the attempt to create authentic "homeplace" in which renewal and recommitment to resistance struggle can take place without a concomitant insistence that members of any community must leave central parts of themselves behind.

Problems of Essentialism in Identity Politics: There is a certain risk in-volved in challenging conceptions of identity. At the time when so many peoples are insisting on speaking in their own voices for the first time, postmodern critiques of the "subject" should indeed be viewed with suspicion.[28] It matters a great deal which voices are heard in the cri-tique. Yet failure to criticize static, essentialized notions of identity serves poorly the task of working toward the possibility of engaging multiple voices in authentic dialogue in which each participant is free to bring her or his entire being.

No one is immune to the effects of racist, sexist, and other stereotypes that are reinforced through the popular media and other societal institu-tions. Canadian singer-songwriter Faith Nolan knows well and expresses powerfully the stereotypes that she must resist:

> I Black woman can barely dance,
> I'd rather read a book than jive and prance,
> I hate wild parties and cheap romance,
> I'm a woman on my own, taking my own stance.
>
> I Black woman will not be used.
> . . . .
> Don't call me your mama, your sister, your girl,
> Don't call me anything in your fantasy world.
> I ain't voodoo queen, an African dream,
> I'm my own woman with my own damn scene.
>
> I Black woman will not be used.[29]

While media images affect diverse groups differently, all are influenced by them to some degree. Patricia Hill Collins describes the different cultural stereotypes of womanhood proffered by dominating culture:

> Within the mind/body, culture/nature, male/female oppositional di-chotomies in Western social thought, objects occupy an uncertain interim position. As objects white women become creations of cul-ture — in this case, uncontrolled female sexuality. In contrast, as animals Black women receive no such redeeming dose of culture and remain open to the type of exploitation visited on nature over-all. Race becomes the distinguishing feature in determining the type of objectification women will encounter.[30]

The construction of race as a category of domination means that the affirmation of blackness, for example, vital in the struggle to affirm self-identified and authentic personhood, must be accompanied by analysis of the ways in which race has been and still is used oppressively. Along with this analysis must come the recognition that no racial or cultural category conveys a unified experience:

> Employing a critique of essentialism allows African-Americans to acknowledge the way in which class mobility has altered collective black experience so that racism does not necessarily have the same impact on our lives. Such a critique allows us to affirm multiple black identities, varied black experience. It also challenges colonial imperialist paradigms of black identity which represent blackness one-dimensionally in ways that reinforce and sustain white supremacy.... Part of our struggle for radical black subjectivity is the quest to find ways to construct self and identity that are oppositional and liberatory.[31]

Rather than abandoning any search for identity, as happens within much postmodern theory, hooks suggests that communities of struggle focus instead on developing that identity that depends not on "essential" characteristics of blackness but rather on historically and politically situated resistance movements.

Lesbian and gay communities are engaged also in heated debates about "identity." Questions about a genetically fixed "homosexual nature" often take precedence over concerted community action to affirm healthy lesbian and gay lifestyles and relationships and to challenge the homophobia and compulsory heterosexism that are still prevalent in dominating society. The idea of such an essentialized identity has a certain appeal to many, particularly those for whom institutional religious and societal approval remains important. Most major religious denominations are patronizingly tolerant of a presumed genetically determined homosexuality that is "more to be pitied than censured."

In Seattle, Washington, a major split occurred over this issue within the local chapter of the national Roman Catholic lesbian and gay organization, Dignity. In response to Vatican demands that Dignity not be permitted to use church facilities, because of the organization's affirmation of the gift of lesbian and gay love, the archdiocese proposed assuming sponsorship of the weekly liturgy held in a Seattle-area church. A major point of conflict, articulated particularly strongly by the women in the organization, was whether acceptance of the archdiocese's offer implied also acceptance of the Vatican's definition of homosexuality as "intrinsically disordered." The offer *was* accepted, the liturgy continues under official sponsorship of the archdiocese's Office of Ministry *to* Gay and Lesbian Persons, and most of the women and many of the men now worship at an alternative location provided by a local Protestant church. The women, perhaps because of their experiences in so many areas of ecclesial and other forms of societal institutions, were more able to identify the "patriarchal outposts in [their] heads" and to refuse a compromise that retained definitions of their reality as lesbians, definitions that were constructed and "disseminated" by sources remote from their own experiences and communities.[32] Those who withdrew have not abandoned their "identity" either as lesbian and gay or as Roman Catholic. They *have* chosen a morally committed oppositional position of resistance to institutional domination, a domination based on an essentialized definition that they understand to be in conflict with their own dignity and agency.[33]

A shift in emphasis beyond unitary identity toward understanding personal and communal multiplicity enables a community to acknowledge the positive and empowering dimensions of its past and present cultural and social reality, without diminishing either the oppressive structures and definitions imposed by the dominating culture or the reality that this oppression is experienced in multiple ways by those differently located within the community. Melanie Kaye/Kantrowitz puts it this way:

> The point of identity politics is not to feel good about ourselves, though this is a necessary and inevitable result. The point is to identify with our own people, however we define this; to struggle with them and bring them along with us, so that we build coalitions which represent a true joining.[34]

Identity politics, historically and culturally situated, while empowering and affirming the positive dimensions of our peoplehood, will also insist that we see our "heelprint upon another woman's face."[35] As Kaye/Kantrowitz acknowledges, "[D]eveloping my identity as a Jew brought me to the Israelis and to the Palestinians."[36] The deconstruction of essentialized notions of identity is not the deconstruction of politics. Rather, this deconstruction "establishes as political the very terms through which identity is articulated."[37] Such a politicized understanding of identity is a necessary lens through which feminist liberation theologians might examine the insights and problems of standpoint theories.

The Promises and Problems of Standpoint as Praxis

The concept of a feminist "standpoint" was developed by Nancy Hartsock in a 1983 article, "The Feminist Standpoint."[38] Although Hartsock has been challenged for inadequate acknowledgment of the reality of multiple locations for women within Western cultures according to the social distinctions structured by race, class, and sexual orientation, her article is useful in delineating some of the features of standpoint epistemology that help in development of a praxis in which multiple diverse voices engage each other.[39] A critical standpoint, which must be achieved rather than inherited with skin color, gender, or other socially evaluated characteristics, allows for the affirmation and acknowledgment of specific socio-historical location and also offers the possibility of movement beyond the limitations of fixed identities.

Using Marxian analyses of the integral relationship of class position with knowledge production, Hartsock insists that material life both structures and sets limits on our understanding of social relations. In addition, in societies structured on oppositional systems of domination, those in power will have a "vision" that is severely limited by its necessary exclusion of perspectives that would challenge the dominating ideology. This vision may not be simply dismissed as "false," however, given its impact on the structures that affect all members of the society. But the more adequate vision that is available to the oppressed group is not one that automatically follows from their social position, but is one that must be struggled for. The achievement of this critical knowledge is attained both by theoretical analysis of the systemic relations that maintain the oppressive structures and by the experience of struggling to resist and overcome these structures. Such a standpoint is an engaged position in which the "real relations between human beings" are exposed as *inhuman,* and alternative possibilities are both envisioned and struggled toward.[40] Thus Hartsock's concept of "standpoint," while developed as an epistemology, incorporates the requirements of transformative praxis in that it suggests both theoretical work and political engagement as necessary components.

Standpoint Praxis and the Privilege of the Oppressed

Implicit in Hartsock's description of an "achieved standpoint" is what has come to be known in liberation discourse as the epistemological privilege of the oppressed. This privilege is not a romanticized conception that somehow bestows automatically on any oppressed group the resources and knowledge necessary to overcome their exploitation and move toward realization of their vision for a more just and humane life. Donna Haraway's description of the complexity of epistemological privilege is helpful:

The standpoints of the subjugated are not "innocent" positions. On the contrary, they are preferred because in principle they are least likely to allow denial of the critical and interpretative core of all knowledge. They are savvy to modes of denial through repression, forgetting, and disappearing acts — ways of being nowhere while claiming to see comprehensively. The subjugated have a decent chance to be on to the god-trick and all its dazzling — and, therefore, blinding — illuminations. "Subjugated" standpoints are preferred because they seem to promise more adequate, sustained, objective, transforming accounts of the world. But *how* to see from below is a problem requiring at least as much skill with bodies and language, with the mediations of vision, as the "highest" techno-scientific visualizations.[41]

Survival in structures that are set up to establish and protect the interests of dominating groups requires that those exploited have, in Haraway's term, a "savvy" about the reality, the lives, and the practices of the dominators. A reverse knowledge is not considered necessary for those who have society's dominant institutions on their side — stereotypes are adequate, indeed vital, to *their* project of exploitation in the service of self-interest. Although the wisdom of those on the "underside" of dominating social institutions has been devalued as not constituting authentic knowledge, it is actually "unexamined dominant [social structures that] are more limiting than others" in terms of what knowledge is made available. The dominant are precluded from authentic knowing because of "their inability to generate the most critical questions about received belief."[42]

These appeals to epistemic privilege, then, are not simple claims for the primacy of a particular "experience." Unexamined experience from *any* location is inadequate in and of itself for the project of dismantling the structures of domination. In addition, it seems clear that oppressive structures will not be transformed without major conversion and significant, critically examined action on the part of many of those who hold such structures in place. The constructive knowledge required to undertake authentically liberating politically engaged action is not a product only of the traditionally recognized educational institutions. Those most deeply involved in the situations to be transformed must participate in the construction of all dimensions of an integrated praxis. Vrinda Dalmiya and Linda Alcoff make a compelling case for the integration of "knowing how" and "knowing that" and insist that "contemporary epistemology needs to recognize that knowledge can be found in unexpected places."[43] Rigoberta Menchú's analysis of the reasons for her people's poverty and suffering and her creativity in finding ways to respond and resist are exemplary of both "knowing how" and "knowing that." Knowledge does indeed emerge from resistance communities as they examine the structures that limit their options and actions in dominating cultural institutional reality.

Standpoint theory makes a major leap from the early days of the current white feminist movement by insisting on "the view [*sic*] from women's lives" rather than undifferentiated "women's experience" as its starting point.[44] This shift is helpful in allowing for a much greater acknowledgment of the profound differences that exist in the women's lives. Yet substituting the term "women's lives" is not sufficient in and of itself. Toinette Eugene points out that the very existence of subjugated knowledge "means that groups are not yet equal in making their standpoints known, either to themselves or to others."[45] The multiple and complex relationships between the lives of diverse women and the ways of making sense of day-to-day experiences require ongoing struggle and dialogue. Is a total relativism the answer, or can standpoint theory avoid the slide into a subjectivist perspective that assumes the equal validity of any praxis and thus eliminates the possibility of ethically committed action?

Objectivity and Socially Situated Knowing

Behind feminist or any other standpoint theory of knowing is the assumption that *all* knowledge projects are socially situated, however explicitly or implicitly, and regardless of the consciousness of this fact on the part of their proponents and adherents. What and how we know both constitute and are constituted by the social, cultural, and political locations of those involved in the construction of knowledge and/or affected by its implementation. Thus there are no stories, in any discipline or time period or context, that are innocent of a certain determination by the cultural and social forces that influence their authors.[46] What feminist standpoint theory insists upon is that its perspectives are *explicitly* politically committed. By naming such a position as "feminist" rather than "women's," feminist practitioners attempt to make clear that their perspective is not and should not be neutral. Patricia Hill Collins calls this "being an advocate for my material" and insists that such a stance is at the heart of her epistemological project of exploring black feminist thought.[47] Such a starting point takes as a given the effects of dominating cultural realities on diverse women's lives and the value of action to overcome that domination.

Objectivity and Objectivism: Accepting the situatedness of all knowledge, and the resultant implication that any particular expression of knowing is at best partial, does not mean the abandonment of all ethical judgment. Neither does it mean a total rejection of the concept of objectivity. Sandra Harding makes a helpful distinction between "strong" and "weak" objectivity and suggests that accepting the partial nature of all knowledge projects, and insisting on increasing inclusion of diverse modes and expressions of knowing, leads to greater and stronger rather than weaker objectivity.[48] It is not that conventional ideas of objectivity are too rigorous, says Harding, but that they are not rigorous enough. Such a position is not objectivity, but *objectivism:*

> Objectivism's rather weak standards for maximizing objectivity make objectivity a mystifying notion, and its mystificatory character is largely responsible for its usefulness and its widespread appeal to dominant groups. It offers hope that scientists and science institutions, themselves admittedly historically located, can produce claims that will be regarded as objectively valid without having to examine critically their own historical commitments from which — intentionally or not — they actively construct their scientific research. It permits scientists and science institutions to be unconcerned with the origins or consequences of their problematics and practices or with the social values and interests that these problematics and practices support.[49]

This objectivism is in direct contrast to standpoint approaches that require the strong objectivity that can take "the subject as well as the object of knowledge to be a necessary object of critical, causal — scientific! — social explanations."[50] The goal thus becomes a project directed toward the construction of *greater* objectivity as the traditional "objects" of knowledge insist upon their "subject" status by their refusal to consider themselves marginal to the development and validation of knowledge.

Feminist unmasking of the old doctrines of objectivity, weak objectivity that excluded the experiences of most of earth's people and posited false universals that reflected only the *un*reflected experience of an elite few, does not eliminate the possibility or need for a reconstructed concept of objectivity that enables us to judge the effectiveness and justice of our collective praxis. Feminist objectivity is rooted in the commitment both to acknowledge as limited any given location and to affirm the validity of situated knowledge. Ethical accountability is central in any project that seeks to deconstruct the idea of a single, hegemonic subject without rendering unimaginable engaged political action by coalitions of diverse persons. Persons committed to increasing the effectiveness of their own knowing emerge from multiple and complex locations within their own as well as the wider culture. Through critical engagement with many others, they recognize through their analysis and resistance struggles the interrelated nature of the domination against which they fight.

The Permanent Instability of Categories: The goal of feminist objectivity, as defined above, is not to search for "the truth." Rather, feminist categories of analysis, and by extension the categories of any theoretical projects, must be seen as permanently "unstable."[51] The kind of objectivity demanded insists upon maintaining awareness of the partial nature of all knowing and the subsequent need for a continual openness to the new insights and shifting images that are the result of the participation of multiple voices in any conversation:

> It would be a delusion for feminism to arrive at a master theory, at a "normal science" paradigm with conceptual and methodological assumptions that we presume all feminists accept. Feminist analytical categories *should* be unstable — consistent and coherent theories in an unstable and incoherent world are obstacles to both our understanding and our social practices.[52]

The problems of essentialized notions of static or rigidly definable "identities" discussed above belie even the *goal* of a metatheory intended to capture either the experiential knowledge of dominated groups or the dynamics of oppression and exploitation used against them.

The lives of all women — indeed, all people — must be seen in what Nancie Caraway calls "deep context."[53] An emphasis on "difference" per se tends to minimize and/or mystify the very real material distinctions in women's lives. The structures behind these differences are illuminated when women's lives, in their specific, nonessentialized, historically positioned locations, are taken seriously. Caraway describes the feminist epistemological project as "feminisms in flux, always already in relations of power." Such feminist theory, which cannot be separated from ethical political commitment and action, draws on the strengths of some dimensions of identity politics, in the service of "empowerment and affirmation of long-silenced hybrid populations," but is significantly different in its insistence on the "incoherencies and contradictions" inherent even within "oppositional identities."[54]

That these identities be oppositional is critical to transformative action, particularly for those who have a historically privileged relationship to a particular context or source:

These shifts in direction transform the academy only if they are informed by nonracist perspective, only if these subjects are approached from a standpoint that interrogates issues of domination and power. A white woman professor teaching a novel by a black woman writer... who never acknowledges the "race" of the characters is not including works by "different" writers in a manner that challenges ways we have been traditionally taught as English majors to look at literature. The political standpoint of any professor engaged with the development of cultural studies will determine whether issues of difference and otherness will be discussed in new ways or in ways that reinforce domination.[55]

It is not only women of relative privilege who must choose an oppositional standpoint. bell hooks, in claiming marginality as a "site of resistance," also insists that clear distinctions must be made between this marginality and that imposed by oppressive structures.[56] The choice of an oppositional standpoint is not one to be made lightly. The transformation required to bring about genuine justice requires change in everyone and a certain willingness to move out of those sometimes rare safe places to which we have retreated for survival:

> The world we have most intimately known, the world in which we feel "safe" (even if such feelings are based on illusions) must be radically changed. Perhaps it is the knowledge that everyone must change, not just those we label enemies or oppressors, that has so far served to check our revolutionary impulses.[57]

Only from these contradictory, oppositional positions will more adequate feminist knowing be produced, knowing that is continually in process of construction as increasingly multiple voices engage in its development. This must include those on the side of privilege. Just as "whites *as whites* can provide traitorous readings of the racial assumptions in texts written by whites," so must women not be "the unique generators of feminist knowledge.... Men must not be permitted to refuse to try to produce fully feminist analyses on the grounds that they are not women."[58] The lives of women currently living within a particular experience continue to have a certain priority and distinctiveness that are not to be subsumed under a notion that, for example, "[A]nyone can produce and develop Black feminist thought."[59] Understanding the relationships between those on both sides of any relationship of domination, however, and holding those on both sides accountable, albeit in different ways, for transforming those relationships in all their complexity must be basic to any liberating theo-ethic.

Questions Raised by Standpoint Theory

Standpoint epistemologies clearly have much to do with the complex identities I highlighted earlier. These theories are not unambiguously helpful in developing approaches to knowledge construction that unmask and demystify the hegemonic structures that hold exploitative practices in place. Many questions arise from consideration of standpoints per se and from the concept of permanent instability, as well as from the complex relationships between experience and identity.

Permanent Instability: Problem or Challenge? The concept of permanent instability is sometimes challenged as precluding adequate theorizing of the overarching structures of power and domination that define many of the relationships in which diverse women live their lives. While acknowledging that attention must be paid to "the differential positioning of women" within societies' exploitative structures, Rosemary Hennessey cautions that "one of the strongest features of feminism's legacy [is] its critique of social totalities like patriarchy and capitalism."[60] In suggesting "instability" as a fundamental characteristic of feminist categories of analysis, Harding thus, according to Hennessey, "forestalls *explanations* of the structures of power to which knowledges are connected and their overdetermined relation to other social practices."[61] Such an emphasis on the instability of theory may lead to further mystification of the fact that multiple social arrangements are interrelated and ultimately lead feminists away from the goal of creating more *adequate* theory.[62]

Harding's work, however, does *not* deny the usefulness of theories but rather stresses that they must be open to change and further development as more and different perspectives are brought into the dialogue that informs them. In calling for rigorous critical analysis rather than mere affirmation of experience, Harding's suggestions indeed *mandate* the theorizing of relationships between and among those who speak and live from diverse and multiply situated standpoints. Disposal of the very project of theorizing is not the only alternative to the ongoing rejection of master narratives that cannot empower groups to work in coalition with each other toward engaged political action.

In much feminist theory, particularly that rooted in spiritual and theological foundations, a search for wholeness has come to imply that there is ultimately some unified oneness that might be achieved if only one works hard enough to "get it right." Nancie Caraway suggests a different interpretation of wholeness gleaned from her readings in black feminist theory. Here, theory is considered holistic "not in the conceit of establishing itself as the universal agent of knowledge for the rest of us...but in the sense of being alert to a *whole world* of potentially violent assaults and entanglements."[63] Here, wholeness has to do with ever-expanding incorporation of every possible diverse perspective and experience, not in the service of discovering some "universal truth," but rather of seeking to clarify points of difference and commonality, and of learning from one another that which our own experiences do not teach. This conception of wholeness as incorporating more and more parts, and so becoming more and more multiple and diverse, is a necessary caution to those who would move too quickly to universalizing categories of either identity or analysis.

What a standpoint approach offers to theoretical endeavors is the continuing challenge to place the real experiences of women's varied lives at the center. White feminist theory may be considered as "action" in and of itself only to the extent that its practitioners refuse to disengage from the political struggles from which their theory emerges and to which it leads. Perhaps one of the major shifts needed in feminist praxis is one beyond the mind-set of either/or and into the both/and as discussed by Patricia Hill Collins:

> Embracing a both/and conceptual stance moves us from additive, separate systems approaches to oppression and toward what I now see as the more fundamental issue of the social relations of domination. Race, class, and gender constitute axes of oppression that characterize black women's experiences within a more generalized matrix of domination. Other groups may encounter different dimensions of the matrix, such as sexual orientation, religion, and age, but the overarching relationship is one of domination and the types of activism it generates.[64]

Donna Haraway sums up the difficult dilemma well: "Our problem is how to have *simultaneously* an account of radical historical contingency for all knowledge claims and knowing subjects...*and* a no-nonsense commitment to faithful accounts of a 'real' world."[65]

Experience, Identity, and Relativism: When the totalizing perspective of any body of theory is challenged, charges of "relativism" abound. The assumption appears to be that, if something is not universally "true," it lacks any validity at all. This is nowhere more evident than in white, Western Christian discourse, and particularly when the exclusivity of Jesus is in question. Yet the attempt to establish a basis for ethical action in cross-cultural perspective emerges in the very books of the Hebrew and Christian scripture, as diverse writers record the very different and sometimes contradictory experiences of their people. Even the development of concepts of the Word reflects efforts to discern how to act ethically in the midst of these multiple voices. Unfortunately, the goal came to be the integration of multiple voices into one dominating, coherent theo-ethical system, a project not possible except through the imposition of sovereign authority.

In the late twentieth century, as the socially constructed and imposed control on all forms of knowing is recognized, the liberal tendency is thus to claim that there *are* no right answers for which to search. All forms of knowing are specific to the individual and thus cannot be judged or evaluated. This posture is deeply problematic in the development of a theo-ethic that seeks justice. The effort to acknowledge diverse perspectives and yet retain the possibility of making both judgments and decisions about ethical praxis is a continuing challenge to feminist scholars. This challenge demands an ability to accept the ambiguous nature of our theo-ethical projects and to recognize that the only way to have absolute answers to our difficult questions is to retreat once again to absolute systems. The choice, it seems, must be to "stand firmly on shifting sand."[66] The search is not for *right answers,* but for *better modes of action.*

In the choice of oppositional standpoints, modes of action are central. Beginning in the reality of one's own and others' lives, shared as discourse that is created and shaped by the very sharing, the dominant systems and perspectives that would place persons in hierarchically ordered relationships with one another come into focus. Questions of relativism and pluralism become less central than does engaged action to overcome situations of oppression and exploitation. Claims to truth are not eliminated in such a praxis. Rather, truths are discerned on the basis of their "explanatory power and...commitment to emancipatory social change."[67] Such claims, because they are recognized to be inextricably enmeshed in particular historical and theoretical frameworks, are open to continuing development and transformation.[68] Adequately understood, a feminist standpoint shifts its claims for authority "from concern over the *grounds* for knowledge — women's lives or experience — to consideration of the *effects* of knowledge as always invested ways of making sense of the world."[69]

The relationships between women's lives and experience, between the differentiated positions women occupy within the same broad cultural, racial, economic, and sexual categories that they inhabit, and between the theoretical constructs that they develop to understand and demystify historical structures of oppression will continue to occupy feminist, womanist, and mujerista theorists in many fields of inquiry. By refusing the separations invoked by rigid modes of knowing, rigid identities, and the often-unintended rigidity of theories that purport to explain more than their participating voices can know, women from diverse socio-historical locations can move together toward a focus on "orthopraxis" rather than "orthodoxy."[70] Surely this criterion affects more than religious understandings and beliefs and applies to the varieties of "truths" with which women engage in the course of their lives. The capacity of any expression or form of knowledge to empower the community and its members in their resistance struggle determines the potential of that knowledge to "do truth."

Beyond Standpoint to Coalition

Coalition often is talked about only in the context of explicit political action. If action, named as resistance struggle against structures of domination, is an integral part of the construction, validation, and expression of knowing for the communities involved, then understandings of coalition must also be expanded to include all aspects of such knowledge production and valorization. The development of a theo-ethic that is committed to hearing and giving voice to multiple standpoints requires engagement in coalition for the production of knowledge in the academy as well as in day-to-day struggle.

The Need for Coalition

Intentional choice of an oppositional location that takes seriously the historically constructed nature of relationships of domination and oppression leads to recognition of the interrelated nature of various modes of exploitation. From the purely practical perspective of numbers, coalition makes sense. June Jordan speaks of the empowerment that can occur when blacks within the United States recognize their oppression as part of a much wider system of racial violence and exploitation. Jordan suggests:

> Rational identification with the First World transforms us — Black folks — from a minority into members of the world's majority, and this means power. This means, for example, that what we are doing now may actually stop the blood run in Central America.[71]

Jordan's creative use of language — reclaiming the term "first world" to apply to those areas inhabited by most of humanity — is yet another way to break through the subtle tyranny exercised by thought patterns "disseminated" to encourage groups of exploited peoples to think of themselves as isolated minorities when, in fact, they constitute the majority of earth's people. Concerted action by strong coalitions is the only effective response to devastating global threats such as the genocidal activity of Western, white Christian groups and governments and the continuing threat of nuclear and ecological "omnicide." While keeping central her commitment to fighting "the slow genocide of poor black women, children, and men," Delores Williams still insists that Christian womanist theologians must "advocate and participate in dialogue and action with *many* diverse social, political, and religious communities concerned about human survival and a productive quality of life for the oppressed."[72]

Retreat into isolated pockets of resistance makes groups more rather than less vulnerable, and accessible to those who believe they have everything to gain by eliminating struggle and awareness on the part of the exploited. Nancie Caraway suggests that "fragmented agents which don't congeal into 'wholes' at certain strategic barricades likely will get vaporized."[73] As some white feminists are coming to acknowledge the historical betrayal by white women of their African-American sisters in the antislavery and suffragist movements, so Caraway notes the ways in which "Black women led the way in articulating the necessity of coalitions for universal human rights."[74] Part of our history that must be recovered is the way in which African-American women initiated movement toward coalition and kept demanding solidarity in the face of continual betrayals. The historical situation of black women was such that coalition with all who will participate was and is crucial. Thus, suggests Caraway,

> We may look to the vision of solidarity and the body of theory which first-wave Black female intellectuals created. The legacy which comes to us in the rich feminism these women created affords a recovery of meaning vital to contemporary feminist thought and politics. The principles of Black abolitionists, suffragists, clubwomen, antilynching activists, and intellectuals redefined the standards of sisterhood and laid the organizational ground for true female solidarity. Theorizing a politics which upheld women's collective efforts toward social change and justice, they created a vision of sisterhood that was based on collective advancement, mutual respect, and individual empowerment.[75]

White feminist erasure of the significance of race and class oppression in the ostensibly generic category of "women's experience" has made those women thus excluded deeply suspicious of attempts at connection. Some of these women, "angered by the insistence on common oppression, shared identity, sameness, criticized or dismissed feminist movement altogether."[76] Yet bell hooks also insists that if she "commits [her]self politically to black liberation struggle, to the struggle to end white supremacy, [she]...must engage in struggle with all willing comrades to strengthen our awareness and our resistance."[77] This engagement is sometimes criticized within African-American communities as assimilationist, but, claims hooks, "[T]here is a grave difference between that engagement with white culture which seeks to deconstruct, demystify, challenge, and transform and gestures of collaboration and complicity."[78] The oppositional consciousness that undergirds authentic solidarity and coalition provides the basis for criteria by which to assess whether given actions are liberatory or assimilationist.

Obviously women from relatively privileged positions have a particular responsibility when engaging in coalition work. Engagement with multiple communities of variously situated persons requires that members of dominant groups take responsibility for their own education about their ambivalent relationships with power structures and with the groups most exploited by those structures. Failure to take this responsibility seriously leads only to further alienation and futile efforts at "inclusion" that frustrate the goal of authentic dialogic praxis among diverse women. We need to go into this work with our eyes and ears wide open. The building of coalition is a difficult and often painful challenge, requiring the development of an oppositional consciousness that is acquired from a position of even relative privilege only through willingness to risk, to make errors and learn from them, and to commit to staying with the process. Reluctance to take the risks involved in joining in struggle with those who have many historical and contemporary reasons for viewing one's participation with skepticism and mistrust is a major factor in hampering movement toward solidarity. Yet oppositional consciousness, achieved through this struggle to know and to risk action, without guarantees of safety or success, is critical to any efforts at solidarity.

Motivating Factors for Coalition

As I suggested earlier, those occupying the most exploited locations in any given culture have little option *but* to engage in coalition wherever they find even minimal willingness to address the issues that threaten the very survival of their communities. The factors that will motivate persons of relatively greater privilege to engage in authentic coalition work are more complex and problematic. I am not speaking here of work in which participants merely insist that others join them in *their* concerns but rather of work that engages us in acknowledging as our own the struggles in which others are engaged. The least helpful of these motivations is guilt. A distinction must be made between "guilt" and accountability.

Feeling guilty about the historical actions of one's people is no automatic guarantee that one will engage in liberative action toward a more just future. Accountability, on the other hand, brings awareness of past injustices, for which one is not personally responsible, into relationship with the privileges one still *receives* from those injustices and thus illuminates one's responsibility to participate in action for change. Knowledge of an oppressive past need not lead to paralyzing guilt. Melanie Kaye/Kantrowitz suggests that "we need to feel our frail/sturdy human hearts outraged by injustice and committed to generosity."[79]

Naming Our Stakes, Choosing Positions: A critical analysis of the oppressive structures that affect people's lives can leave those whose survival is not immediately threatened feeling helpless because of the magnitude of "it all," or such analysis can motivate them to action by enabling them to see that structures that are *man*-made can be *un*made. And acknowledgment of one's relationship with and accountability for those structures can lead to the envisioning of new possibilities. South African activist Ruth First, when questioned about her own motivation for engaging as a white woman in antiapartheid struggle in her country, replied that she was "not a white fighting for the blacks, but a person fighting for her own right to live in a just society."[80] This recognition of a common goal — a just society — is what may inspire individuals and communities beyond guilt and into joining other struggles as their own. The history of betrayal between such groups as white and African-American women is such that no instant, easy trust is available in such work. Yet waiting until this "trust" is established is not an option. Those who know their own and their children's and families' lives to be at stake are not interested in sitting around talking about trust; orthopraxis is the criterion for evaluation:

> If we could start working together *before* we trust, understand, or like each other, we might learn to.... We have gotten entirely too theoretical about these issues, expecting that with words, with ideas, we can work it all out in advance. Perhaps we need to engage, even in uncertainty, and work out issues as they arise.[81]

White women committed to engaging in antiracist activity do well to heed Barbara Smith's caution: "White women don't work on racism to do a favor for someone else. . . . You have to comprehend how racism distorts and lessens your own lives as white women."[82]

The *choice* of location and oppositional consciousness does not apply only to those on the more privileged side of relationships of domination. People from any socio-historical location are vulnerable to the stereotypes and myths perpetuated by dominating society, and all need to come to a level of recognition of the constructed nature of these myths and images in order to engage in oppositional resistance. As an example, bell hooks examines the ways in which some feminist theory tends to suggest that women are "by nature" more caring and peace-oriented because of their biological capacity to bear children. On the contrary,

> Many women who mother (either as single parents or in camaraderie with husbands) have taught male children to see fighting and other forms of violent aggression as acceptable modes of communication, modes that are valued more than loving or caring interaction. . . . *We must insist that women who do choose (even if they are inspired by motherhood) to denounce violence and domination and its ultimate expression, war, are political thinkers making political decisions and choices.*[83]

One has only to recall the militarism of Margaret Thatcher, and the tenderness with which many gay men tend one another and others in the AIDS crisis, to find immediate examples of the inadequacy of a position based on an *essential* linking of women with nurturing and men with violence.[84] In addition, such a proposition continues to tend toward placing sole responsibility for the care and nurturing of children, and other human beings, as well as care of the earth and resistance to war, in the hands of women.[85] By contrast, women and men who resisted the devastating reality of slavery *chose* their positions in opposition to their existential reality:

> Understanding marginality as position and place of resistance is crucial for oppressed, exploited, colonized people. If we only view the margin as sign marking the despair, a deep nihilism penetrates in a destructive way the very ground of our being. . . . These margins have been both sites of repression and sites of resistance. And since we are well able to name the nature of that repression we know better the margin as site of deprivation. We are more silent when it comes to speaking of the margin as site of resistance.[86]

In this dimension of *choice* lies the possibility of redefining "the margin" as a space of resistance and hope rather than merely a space of despair, and thus choice opens up ways of moving within that space to connect with others inhabiting differently defined but related "margins."

In choosing margins as spaces of resistance, communities of struggle defy the validity and authority of the "center" that has defined relationships of domination. Perhaps the image of a web works better, where many "margins," each with its own central standpoint, intersect with each other. I have in mind something similar to Nancie Caraway's "crossover tracks [which enable movement] back and forth to coalitions and affinity spaces,"[87] or singer-songwriter Marsie Silvestro's "line-crossing":

> I'm crossing the lines for justice,
> I'm crossing the lines for peace;
> I'm crossing the lines for liberation,
> I'm crossing the lines for you.
> Bread lines, picket lines, border lines, life lines...[88]

In order to maintain the integrity of the historical relations between and among those "crossing over" such boundary spaces, white feminists need to keep alive a politics of memory. In doing so, stories are told of "segregated sisterhood," and accountability is acknowledged for "those silences which denied the feminist spirit of countless poor, working-class, lesbian, Black, and other women of color."[89] Nonessentialized identification with a particular historical location, when integrated with authentic commitments to life together in a creatively imagined just society, might empower multiply situated women to work together toward just such a goal.

Valuing Differences: There are two important points to keep in mind when discussing the value and significance of "differences." First, there is the distinction between, on one hand, different social locations that are imposed by unjust institutionalized structures of oppression and, on the other hand, the differing experiences of persons who must live within those structures, only some of which are determined by the structures. Second, when I suggest that the valuing of differences is a motivating factor for engaging in coalition work with multiply situated persons and communities, I do not want to give credence to romanticized views of the "exotic other." Rather, I suggest an increasing awareness that cultural, political, and other knowing is incomplete and impoverished to the extent that it lacks critical engagement with the knowings acquired and valued in other contexts. Understanding differences as rich resources for the deepening of personal integrity is an attempt to resist the hierarchical problematizing of "difference" imposed by hegemonic systems of control and offers the possibility for creative action.

Drawing from a lifetime of experiences in which conceptions of differences posed both problems and resources for creativity, Audre Lorde suggests:

> Too often, we pour the energy needed for recognizing and exploring difference into pretending those differences are insurmountable barriers, or that they do not exist at all. This results in a voluntary isolation, or false and treacherous connections. Either way, we do not develop tools for using human difference as a springboard for creative change within our lives. We speak not of human difference, but of human deviance.[90]

Difference is seen frequently as suspect, particularly when it appears to threaten the unity of a community. But, insists Lorde, "[T]he need for unity is often misnamed as a need for homogeneity."[91] When unity is understood in terms of solidarity, coming together to make one's own the interrelated struggles in which we are all engaged, then diverse experiences — differences in positionality — offer multiple creative resources for necessary action. The acknowledgment and acceptance of differences require moving from an understanding of difference as posing "a threat to the 'common denominator' category."[92] Perhaps when questions of "difference" can be approached with an integrated perspective that acknowledges both the problematic, oppressive dimensions of relationships of domination *and* the rich creative cultural and political resources diverse communities and individuals have to offer each other, white women will be able to avoid both immersion in "guilt" and a fascination with things "other" — both of which continue dominating practices by co-optation rather than promoting integrated engagement with such resources.

Barriers to Coalition

There are many limiting factors that make coalition-building a difficult and dangerous proposition. I mention just three that are particularly problematic to those who enjoy varying degrees of unearned privilege and who choose — or at least *want* to choose — an oppositional consciousness that moves them to action in solidarity with women (and men) whose own beginning standpoint may be different from their own.

The Problematic Character of Liberal Pluralism: Liberal conceptions of pluralism are rooted in white, Western individualism that places the rights of each individual (usually, in practice, the rights of individual white, heterosexual men of economic privilege) ahead of any communal good. Those who have long been able to count on such protection of individual rights — because their own viewpoints are those validated by society's "norms" — are those who express the fear that pluralism will degenerate into a situation where judgments of ethical value cannot be made because all viewpoints must be considered equally valid.

Embracing "pluralism" abstractly, without the historical contextualization necessary to choosing an oppositional location, is totally inadequate if one's objective is the transformation of structures that define and maintain oppressive relationships with those who are "different":

> Some white people who take up multicultural and cultural plurality issues mean well, but often they push to the fringes once more the very cultures and ethnic groups about whom they want to disseminate knowledge. For example, the white writing about Native peoples or cultures displaces the Native writer and often appropriates the culture instead of proliferating information about it. The difference between appropriation and proliferation is that the first steals and harms; the second helps heal the breach of knowledge.[93]

Canadian writer Anne Cameron, whose work has included the publishing of stories of the Nootka people of Vancouver Island, Canada, offers an example of the possibility of moving beyond a liberal pluralist approach.[94] Cameron recently agreed to a request from Canadian First Nations women writers to put her influence into assisting them in getting their own work published, instead of continuing to record and publish the stories herself.

Focusing only on pluralism and diversity, and the "multiculturalism" that Gloria Anzaldúa identifies as "a euphemism for the imperializing and now defunct 'melting pot,' "[95] does nothing in and of itself to dismantle the systems of racist and economic oppression. These structures remain mystified without a material, historical commitment to analysis of the many factors that constitute the "differences" encountered.

Tokenism: Related to liberal pluralism is the tokenism to which attempts at inclusion often fall prey. One of the worst forms of tokenism evidenced by academicians is the use of materials from differently situated communities without either addressing adequately one's own historical relationships with the community involved or allowing the insights gained from the materials to substantively change one's very methodology. Rosemary Hennessey appreciates "the ways in which multicultural studies rewrite the universalized Eurocentric subject of humanist knowledge," but claims that

> [t]he new knowledge it offers also needs critical attention from its supporters, attention that is vigilant to the many subtle ways in which university reforms can rewrite and suppress the oppositional force of counterhegemonic knowledges....
>
> To the extent that diversity courses attend to cultural differences without questioning how difference organizes knowledge and how this organization is in turn imbricated in larger social structures, they can serve as one of the academy's most skillful crisis *management* strategies.[96]

In order for these courses to function in oppositional ways, those teaching such material must move beyond "celebrating or appreciating difference" and insist that both they and their students acquire "the critical frameworks to understand how and why social differences are reproduced."[97]

Another demonstration of tokenism is the current practice of seeking the spokesperson for any particular group to "address" the issue with which she or he is identified in the eyes of the audience, academic institution, church body, and so forth. Speaking on a panel in a women's studies conference, Audre Lorde addressed directly the tokenization she experienced:

> It is a particular academic arrogance to assume any discussion of feminist theory without examining our many differences, and without a significant input from poor women, Black and Third World women, and lesbians. And yet, I stand here as a Black lesbian feminist, having been invited to comment within the only panel at this conference where the input of Black feminists and lesbians is represented.[98]

One of the effects of such tokenism is that it puts diverse communities of struggle in competition with each other, as well as placing in the hands of the dominant group the power to determine who will represent the community. Movement beyond tokenism must mean the refusal of dominant/dominating groups to maintain control over who will speak and how. White women, for example, must demonstrate in word and action their seriousness about more than a peripheral commitment to engaged and sustained conversation, and often confrontation, with those whose voices have yet to be heard in contexts such as that referred to by Lorde.

Fear of Anger and Hostility: For white, privileged women from many Western cultural locations, particularly those who have been well "Christianized," anger has long been an emotion fraught with fear and tension. They have learned that anger is not acceptable and that it is a fearful thing that, once unleashed, may be totally uncontrollable. Women's experiences of violence at the hands of their predominantly male lovers, spouses, and fathers have only exacerbated this fear. Until such violations are systematically analyzed from the perspective of the oppositional consciousness mentioned above, and can finally be understood not as the inevitable result of disagreement or difference of opinion but as part of a strategy of maintaining control, women will turn from the empowering potential of justified rage.

In her extraordinary essay "The Power of Anger in the Work of Love," Beverly Harrison is eloquent in her reclamation of anger as a powerful and necessary resource in the work of making justice:

> Where anger rises, there the energy to act is present. In anger, one's body-self is engaged, and the signal comes that something is amiss in relation. To be sure, anger — no more than any other set of feelings — does not lead automatically to wise or humane action. . . . We must never lose touch with the fact that all serious human moral activity, especially action for social change, takes its bearings from the rising power of human anger. Such anger is a signal that change is called for, that transformation in relation is required.[99]

Melanie Kaye/Kantrowitz raises some important issues when she asks why women continue to see rage, hatred, and even violence as unthinkable against "men who abuse and . . . men who do nothing to stop this abuse."[100] Kaye/Kantrowitz is not advocating simple resort to violence as a solution, but she asks provocative questions about how we might "hang on to our own anger, hatred even, long enough . . . but no longer."[101] The relationship of anger to violence is one that needs further critical analysis by feminist/womanist/mujerista theo-ethicists, analysis that is beyond the scope of the present book.

The "anger, hatred even" they encounter or perceive can prevent women *and* men from willingly engaging in critical encounters where they may ultimately be able to move this passionate energy to constructive action. bell hooks speaks of "black female rage towards white women" as

> [a] rage rooted in the historical servant-served relationship where white women have used power to dominate, exploit, and oppress.

Many black women share this animosity, and it is evoked again and again when white women attempt to assert control over us. This resistance to white female domination must be separated from a black female refusal to bond with white women engaged in feminist struggle.[102]

The confrontations that emerge from that anger that is sign and symbol of distortions in relationships between and among members of diverse groups do not inevitably lead to violence and destruction. As hooks notes elsewhere, "[W]omen need to have the experience of working through hostility to arrive at understanding and solidarity if only to free ourselves from the sexist socialization that tells us to avoid confrontation because we will be victimized or destroyed."[103] Confrontation and hostility are inevitable products of systems of domination and exploitation. Such systems cannot be transformed without those most affected by them engaging one another seriously enough to move through this rage in ways that harness its energy into creativity for action.

In July of 1992, at a national conference of women of faith in Spokane, Washington, American Indian activist Marilyn James shared her current efforts for the retrieval and burial of the remains of her ancestors. James's people, the Sinixts, lived in the Arrow Lakes region of what is now known as British Columbia, Canada, before being dispersed by the same colonizing tactics used throughout the continent when prime land was commandeered by European settlers. This dispersal left the tribe with no central "home" from which to fight the Canadian government's 1956 decision to declare them "extinct," thus rendering them ineligible for any consideration in issues of land or other rights. James related how another group, the Okanagans, "was willing to step up to the plate and offer us existence because they understood the importance of getting our ancestors back."[104] Although their own "plate was full" with the struggles besetting their own nation, the Okanagan tribal council knew well the need for coalition if justice was to be achieved even in small measure for anyone.

For the Sinixts, as for others whose voices are refused a hearing in the structures of powerful political systems, coalition with the Okanagans helped in their search for some small measure of justice from the government. The Okanagans, immersed in struggles of their own over land rights, knew that the integrity of their own struggles was dependent upon their capacity to honor and lend strength — in this case, the strength of official recognition — to the struggle of their sisters and brothers. A sense of community, of "homeplace," is of critical importance for those whose sense of self is derogated by the dominant cultural norms and mores of society. At the same time, essentialist interpretations of identity limit the effectiveness of communities in engaging in necessary resistance struggle. Crossing boundaries of identity may ensure the survival and enhance the quality of life of both Sinixts and Okanagans. Many of the basic premises of standpoint theory are helpful in allowing for complex, socially constituted identities that are not rigidly defined but enable recognition of both oppressive and empowering points of connection. These connections invite theo-ethicists seeking a praxis of justice into the ambiguity and struggle of coalition, in all phases of their work. The resulting solidarity may have the capacity to move all of us beyond tokenism, fragmentation, and liberal pluralism into a genuine chorus of diverse voices.

The wisdom and multiple expressions of knowing that abound in diverse communities mandate the incorporation of their "voices" in theo-ethical discourse. Women like Marilyn James create and embody knowledge that empowers survival and quality of life in situations of struggle and violence, deprivation and isolation. Women differently positioned within any given community offer diverse knowings that amplify each other's perspective. Because of the global nature of the systems that maintain oppression and violation, we cannot afford the dubious luxury and false security of remaining within the boundaries of our own particular community or identity, however we define it. No one individual or group can speak *the* Word of truth to or for all others. Each does, however, have *words* that others must hear, whether through song or poetry, autobiography or visual art, SF or theoretical explorations.

The approach to knowledge production and validation outlined here does not bear much resemblance to the ways in which religious dogma has been "disseminated" to the faithful through the ages. What difference might it make to those central tenets of white, Western, masculinist theological discourse if the incarnation of the sacred in history, in which Christians say they believe, also speaks through diverse and multiple locations and constructions? If religious knowing truly cannot be separated from other modes of knowing, how might serious attention to diverse voices change our basic conceptions of the divine?

Chapter 6

Voices of Struggle,
Echoes of God

If we are going to recognize the "echoes of God" that are articulated through "voices of struggle," then we must elaborate some methods for hearing those voices. Throughout this book, I have claimed that a metaphor of many voices assists in developing a theo-ethical praxis in which multiply diverse participants work together to express with greater integrity the continuing revelation of the sacred in the world. Listening to varied expressions of those voices — in autobiography, poetry, song, SF, and theo-ethical and other theory — raises both methodological and theo-ethical issues that are a continuing challenge to those whose primary site of theo-ethical explorations is the academy but who retain a commitment to the increase of justice in their own and other lands. Some of these issues I have raised already. In this concluding chapter, I propose some specific implications of this metaphor for theo-ethical education and discourse and discuss some ways in which a metaphor of many voices challenges our conceptions of the divine.

Methodological Challenges

I have suggested that a coalitional praxis is central to theo-ethical discourse, just as it is to more overtly political work. This approach demands a radical shift in the ways in which formal theo-ethical education is undertaken. Adding "people of color" to faculties and/or student bodies is, in and of itself, inadequate, unless the presence of multiply situated persons with diverse experiences changes the praxis of the institution. I cited both relationship and the transformation of method as primary criteria when privileged scholars approach texts from communities with which they have historical connections of unjust and unequal power. These same criteria apply to institutions that endeavor to move toward more integrity in their attempts at inclusiveness and diversity. Mutual relationships cannot, by definition, be unilateral. Interactions between and among the two or more parties, when truly engaged, change all those involved.

Neither adding the occasional book by one who is not a white, Western, masculinist scholar nor refusing to do so on the grounds that one cannot fully understand materials from another culture are adequate responses to the need for authentic dialogue across the lines of differences. Those who have happily engaged the works of Shakespeare, Goethe, Paul, and the prophets of the Hebrew Bible have seldom claimed that they could not teach diverse texts because they were unfamiliar with the context from which the materials arose. Courage is required here — willingness to risk charges of co-optation and misappropriation and to learn from our mistakes, when these charges are well founded; commitment to face honestly the injuries of racism, sexism, classism, heterosexism, and so forth, which damage our capacities to relate honestly with one another; determination to uncover the ways in which we knowingly and unknowingly perpetuate the very systems that uphold unjust relations.

In addition, the definition of what counts as "text" must change. The term "text" is derived from the Latin *textus,* meaning texture, context, and from *textere,* to weave. The con-text in which we live includes music, art, poetry, and other literature. This context embraces the engaged lives of students and faculty and administrators and staff, and those with whom they interact in their families, communities, parishes, and justice organizations; those we read about in the news or whose absence from the news should give us pause; those who hold out their cups as we pass by on the streets; the water we drink and the air we breathe and the ground upon which we walk. All these and many more provide the text — the context — for our theo-ethical explorations.

The criteria I have suggested for evaluating the praxis of white feminist theo-ethicists of relative privilege are but starting points for critical self-evaluation that tends toward transformative and hopeful change rather than paralyzing self-deprecation. These criteria will be assessed as more or less adequate to the extent to which they challenge movement toward a theo-ethical context that does indeed do more than talk about "difference" and "inclusivity." There are risks involved in undertaking this work, not the least of them the acknowledgment that one's own work falls far short of the demands of authentic multivocal discourse even as one advocates it as vital to the promotion of justice. Yet only by moving despite our fears, engaging one another despite our perceived inadequacies — raging and weeping and laughing and screaming and loving through the conflicts and defeats as well as in the small victories — can we hope to move beyond fragmentation and frustration into genuinely empowering solidarity.

An Articulate God: Word or Voices?

Issues of authority have risen in multiple contexts as feminist writers and other activists have attempted to challenge the prevailing white, Western, masculinist paradigm in ways which enable multiple voices to speak and be heard. The overidentification of sovereign authority with written text has led to rigid interpretations of "Word" that are manifest in contemporary religious contexts as the authoritarian institutions of Protestant biblicism and Roman Catholic magisterialism. The concept of God that emerges from these interpretations is less of the God who speaks than of one who has spoken or is spoken for — represented — in and by those with the authority to do so. A metaphor of many voices, rather than Word, suggests that the holy does indeed still speak, give voice to ongoing revelation in the lives of the many who have been unheard and/or actively silenced — often in the name of the very God who is thus represented. I do not suggest that we discard all notions of "Word," or scripture, or church. Rather, a metaphor of voices assists in reinterpreting our relationship with each other and with all individuals and institutions with whom and which we interact and thus transforms our understandings of authority.

Authority as sovereignty must give way to understandings of authority as "an augmentation of the texture of daily life."[1] Action that enhances the day-to-day life of persons struggling for dignity and justice within their multiple locations and communities determines the criteria for what is considered authoritative. Onnie Lee Logan's authority to practice midwifery came from the need of the women in her area who knew that if they sent for the doctor, "[T]he baby woulda been there and probably some of em walking befo' he got there."[2] If Logan needed any legitimation of the authenticity of her call, it came through the success of her efforts to enhance the well-being of the women and infants with whom she worked. Bettina Aptheker speaks of the enormous expression of resistance that inheres in the "dailiness of women's lives."[3] The silent and subtle ways in which women exercise their own form of authority in terms of their capacity to "augment and make increase" the quality of life for entire families and communities constitute powerful resistance strategies.

Renewed understandings of authority imply new interpretations of leadership. We are accustomed to images of a "charismatic ruler [who] lives above and beyond the masses he inspires."[4] What is required is recognition and affirmation of that leadership described by Kathleen Jones as "a practice for establishing networks that sustain connections."[5] As Rigoberta Menchú observes, "[T]he role of a leader is as a coordinator.... [T]he struggle is propelled forwards by the *compañeros* themselves."[6] The authority of this leadership, emerging from and validated by the community, is evaluated in terms of its effects on the community as a whole. Orthopraxis is central. The "truth" does indeed reside in that which sets free.

The leadership suggested here does not "represent" the interests of the community. This leadership is, rather, articulated from *within* the community, even when particular designated spokespersons are giving voice to explicit concerns. Chung Hyun Kyung uses the image of "echo" to suggest the role of the academically trained theologian in promoting the justice struggles of her people. "Echoes are the most honest and powerful testimony to the poor woman's voice of truth" until that day arrives when the echo will change into a "symphony in which every woman, regardless of background,... is able to make her own sound of truth heard."[7]

Conceptions of an omnipotent deity, represented to humankind through self-proclaimed agents of holy power, do not serve well the development of authentic agency in God or in humans as cocreators of just and meaningful life. A God who is the first and last Word — and must rely upon official representatives to enforce "his" decrees, either through rigid interpretations of scripture or through equally rigid adherence to the Word of "his" church — is not the God who empowered Onnie Lee Logan to trust and employ her own motherwit, or Rigoberta Menchú to become an international spokesperson on behalf of justice for her people and for indigenous peoples everywhere. The God of Menchú, Logan, and others might better be named "omni-articulate," in light of the diverse ways in which sacred presence has been revealed to these women and disclosed through their lives. A move from *representation* to *articulation* in understanding human relationships with the sacred provides the possibility of renewed relationships among all beings who share this earth-home, in the context of their association with the divine.

When I began to think about "articulation" as a mode of understanding the relationship between God and humans and other earth creatures, I was aware of the variety of different meanings that adhere to the term. As a child, I understood that to *articulate* meant to speak clearly, in such a way that the sounds were meaningful to those who were listening. At the same time, my British story and picture books referred to those vehicles that I now call "semis" as "articulated lorries." Later, I discovered that "articulate" meant not only clarity of diction but also the coherency with which one expresses ideas.

What do these rather diverse meanings have in common? The root of the word "articulate" means "joint," and the term has, at different points in time, been applied to the joining point of two parts and to the parts themselves. In the present context, I suggest that the significance of this concept is in its emphasis on the *relationship* of the parts. An "articulated lorry" — a semi — is efficient and effective inasmuch as its distinct but connected parts retain a relationship such that they work together to convey freight; this image can provide a reminder that "articulation" is not a concept limited to the spoken or written word. Similarly, words are effective according to how well they are constructed, joined, and given voice in order to convey meaning. There is no disputing the effectiveness of the articulations of Rigoberta Menchú, Onnie Lee Logan, and Audre Lorde. But what might it mean to insist that God is "articulate(d)"?

An adequate exploration of the implications of a concept of articulation for understanding the doctrine of God might be a study in itself and is beyond the scope of my project at this time. Here, I am concerned with the implications of this shift in emphasis — from a God who is Word to one who speaks through the "voices" of all created being — for a theo-ethical enterprise in which those steeped in the theologies of white, Western, masculinist Christianity might engage in authentic and nonexploitative dialogue with others whose voices are central in this study. There are three major characteristics of an "articulate(d) God" that I believe are central to such a project. First, God speaks, clearly, in a manner in which it is possible for listeners to hear and understand and does not require the mediation of "representatives." Second, this God is not a unitary being but can more accurately be understood as the movement in the "joints" that maintain the connections between the diverse elements of God-bearing (incarnate) reality. Third, the "articulations" of God are not directed toward some ultimate and undifferentiated oneness but rather retain their distinctiveness even as they enter more and more deeply into profound relationship.

God as Speaker

In insisting that God speaks, now and historically and in the future, I return to the heart of my claim that "voice(s)" more adequately reflect(s) the activity of God in the world than do static conceptions of Word.

Donna Haraway makes important distinctions between articulation and representation and suggests some of the dynamics that work against the interests of large numbers of earth's creatures in a politic of representation.[8] Haraway points out that representation depends upon an act of distancing between the representative and the represented, as well as between the represented and her/his/its context. Using the examples of the jaguar in the rain forests of Latin America, and of the fetus in reproductive technology debates, Haraway argues that in both cases, questions of "who speaks for" the jaguar and the fetus are misleading and ultimately destructive of a process in which all affected entities might be involved in resolving the issues at stake. Scientific approaches of representation isolate the "object" of concern from its context. Those who are most closely involved — in these examples, the Kayapó Indians and the rain forest itself, and pregnant women — are considered the least able to participate in decision-making because of their nonobjectivity.[9]

Important in the current context of discussion about God is Haraway's use of the image of "ventriloquist" to describe the ways in which "representatives" claim to speak *for* those whom they identify as the objects of their concern, whether those "objects" be jaguars and Kayapó Indians, fetuses and pregnant women, or human communities and God. The assumption that such "objects" cannot represent themselves renders them forever without their own voices and in need of the services of a ventriloquist.[10] The jaguar, fetus, and community, along with their protagonists, are reduced to "the permanent status of the recipient of action, never to be a co-actor in an articulated practice among unlike, but joined, social partners."[11] This is a concept diametrically opposed to Chung's suggestion mentioned earlier of the theo-ethicist acting as "echo" until the oppressive dynamics of silencing are transformed in order that all may "speak" on their own behalf. A metaphor of voices, situated in Haraway's understanding of articulation, challenges the right of anyone to speak *for* another, whether that other be human, other-than-human, and/or divine. Rather, ways must be explored in which created beings, human and other, may hear each other as "echoes" of sacred voice and engage in coalition and solidarity to enhance the well-being of their individual and communal contexts.

Haraway's exposition of representation resonates with conceptions of sovereign authority. Theologians and fathers of the church take on the role that Haraway sees ascribed to scientists, that of representing the sacred to "their" people, and "their" people to the sacred. The Word of God, expressed in the Bible or through church institutions, takes on an authority that must rely upon coercion for its implementation. This coercion is seldom as overtly violent in contemporary Christianity as it was in such atrocities as the Spanish Inquisition, medieval witch-hunts, or colonization efforts around the world. Yet women who have suffered violent abuse at the hands of males, for example, know all too well how the Bible has been used by clerics and others to convince battered women that it is their "Christian duty" to remain in abusive situations.[12] Roman Catholic clergy and religious who are "called" to public office, or who take pro-choice positions regarding reproductive freedoms, experience the authoritarian Word of the church in coercive actions against them.[13]

Many women who have survived abuse, both in their families and in their churches, have claimed their *own* authority and, together with the other women heard in this study, have begun to embody Haraway's conception of articulation. Such a concept has much in common with the Sophia/Wisdom tradition in which the dynamic relationship of God and human is central and the significance of human thought and action more consistently affirmed. In refusing to be "represented" by others, and similarly by refusing the representation of what constitutes God, sin, grace, salvation, or the kingdom (*sic*) of God by those who do not share their own particular situation, women have continued throughout history to author their lives in the context of their communities, sustained by the personal and communal articulations of the sacred that they encounter there. In the "voices" of these women, regardless of the modes of expression, God speaks.

The God who has spoken to people through the ages, and in particular to the women whose experiences are recounted here, is nothing if not creative in terms of the manner of communication chosen. When I use the term "speech," I use it in a wide sense rather than in its limited definition of the vocalized sound patterns of structured language. An articulate God has been experienced as speaking directly to individuals, as in the case of the women preachers; through the elements of the created world; through the needs of exploited neighbors and friends and selves. Communities of survival and struggle have devised creative ways to communicate in, through, and around the imposed language of the masters. Through those who have heard and embodied this communication, God has spoken in ways that have led to their resistance to structures of oppression and to the ongoing survival of their people.

Clearly, not all who claim to be bearing the voice of God are seen to be working to *increase* the degree of justice in the world. The development of criteria for self-evaluation of the orthopraxis of individuals and communities is an urgent and continuing challenge. Yet the concept of articulation does assist, I believe, in enabling us to affirm the voices of God, persistent in the midst of structures of oppression and exploitation. While questioning the adequacy of a once-and-for-all-time and exclusive embodiment of divinity in the person of Jesus, I do take very seriously the Christian claim that God is incarnate in material reality. Thus God must speak, if at all, from that place of embodiment and in the voice to which any given creature, human or other, has access. An adequate interpretation of incarnation suggests that God is not merely represented in materiality but is articulate(d) there. Thus the questions that must be addressed are those of uncovering the multitudinous ways in which God's articulation is made manifest and of exploring modes of communication between and among highly differentiated entities.

God as Communities in Solidarity

One of the major motivating factors in the establishment of "Word" as a primary metaphor in Judeo-Christian history was the perceived need to assert monotheism in unambiguous and authoritative terms. Even the concept of Sophia/Wisdom, cast in female language, was seen as threatening to the One God of both Jewish and early Christian tradition.[14] In the early christological debates, when the nature of the divine/human relationship in the person of Jesus was at issue, the groundwork was laid for the later development of a trinitarian doctrine that would take the place of Sophia/Wisdom in attempting to address the existential experience of a divine reality that could not be contained in a static, unified, male oneness.

Some Christian-feminist theologians have turned to trinitarian concepts to challenge exclusive emphasis on the maleness of God. María Clara Bingemer describes the Trinity as "a community of love between persons...where the differences and pluralities are not suppressed but integrated."[15] Although Bingemer frames her thesis in the problematic terms of "masculine" and "feminine," with their implicit suggestion of essentialized male and female natures that are not derived from social forces, her point is well taken that trinitarian doctrine does indeed possess some potential for the integration of "pluralism, change, and difference" into what she sees as the "divine unity."[16] Most significant in Bingemer's exposition is her claim that understanding the mystery of the Trinity as a mystery of relationships in community means that "a lone individual cannot be the image of this God insofar as he or she is open to relationship and communitarian being."[17]

Although trinitarian doctrine has potential for advancing a certain element of relationality within what is understood to be the reality of

God, it is not adequate to encompass the radical diversity of beings through and in whom an articulate divinity speaks. Underlying any current understanding of trinitarian doctrine is the assumption that at bottom, God is one and unified, the source of an original unity from which emerged all that is, and to which all will return. The sacred power — the authentic authority — of any myth or belief is in its capacity to explain contemporary and historical reality and to move its adherents to continue to struggle for full and just life together on the earth. Historical and contemporary experiences of dislocation, forced relocation, and genocide mean that claims to a unified myth of origin have limited capacity to explain the distorted and unequal relationships that adhere among multiple communities today. Still less do such experiences, particularly as they have continued in Eastern Europe, Africa, the Middle East, Northern Ireland, and the inner cities of the United States, suggest that humankind, much less the rest of creation, is moving toward this utopic oneness.

Octavia Butler's *Xenogenesis* SF series is exemplary of a different metaphor, one potentially more empowering because of its rootedness in the existential reality of complex and varied identities. Butler's trilogy is situated in a post–nuclear holocaust time, when the remaining humans are rescued by, and dependent on, alien beings for their continued reproduction. Movement into greater diversity and complexity, rather than unity, is what will maintain the ongoing viability of both the humans and the Oankali. Butler's work echoes Delores Williams's suggestion that survival and quality of life are central in African-American women's struggles, historically and in the present. The *Xenogenesis* example is better described as "survival fiction" than as the salvation history that has been the dominant literary metaphor.[18] Butler's work thus suggests a more realistic metaphor — one rooted in authentic possibility and so more empowering of action and hope — than is an image of an original and ultimate unity in which differences will be subsumed. Butler's premise is not dissimilar from that which is currently being discovered in ecological science. Replantings of forests in the wake of strip-logging operations, where these plantings have supplied only a limited number of species of trees — those most lucrative for future logging operations — have not served to preserve the environment. The *diversity* of the original forest is essential to its ongoing viability.

Just as no one human being can be conceived of (or conceived) in total isolation or understood in simplistic terms of a mono-identity, so must our understandings of the sacred be expanded to allow for the diversity and multiplicity inherent in a God who is articulate in all the splendid multivalences of creation.

God as Movement in Connection

A God who is speaking in the multiple voices of diverse persons and other earth creatures cannot be defined as a static being. Neither does it seem satisfactory to conceive of God as endlessly scattered, embodied in multiple images and definitions that relate poorly if at all to each other. Current attempts to image God as female as well as male, as black as well as white, as poor as well as affluent, are helpful initially in empowering persons to see themselves as imaging such a God. Ultimately, however, they are limited by the same potential for exclusivity and essentialist conceptions of both God and humans as is identity politics.[19]

The ability to conceive of oneself as reflecting the sacred is a critical first step away from a rigid Word who, once spoken, is forever to be understood in one static image, carefully interpreted by "his" representatives. Recognizing that same reflection in persons different from ourselves in one or many aspects of our personhood might lead us to acknowledge the dynamism of a God who cannot be "caught" in any static image or symbol. A recognition of God as "our power in relation to each other, all humanity, and creation itself" has potential to offer us the opportunity to encounter God in our struggles for dialogue and coalition.[20] Given the shifting dynamics of all relationships, such a God may not be "captured" but can nevertheless be known as constantly moving — and moving us, when we hear authentically both our own voices and those of the others with whom we are engaged — toward transformation of the multiple dimensions of our connections with each other.

In a world marked by relationships fractured by inequitable power dynamics, the transformation of such relationships demands both recognition and analysis of the complex injustices involved. In much current discussion, the term "privilege" is used in an effort to denote awareness of the unearned rewards that accrue to persons on the basis of skin color, economic status, gender, sexual orientation, and a host of other characteristics. While an understanding of the unearned nature of such rewards is an important dimension of overcoming exploitation, such awareness is valuable only to the extent to which it motivates and empowers movement into greater justice and equality.[21] This movement may consist in a commitment on the part of a white student to take response/ability[22] for challenging racist comments from professors or other students; the endeavors of a man and woman to move beyond established gender norms in their relationship; the decision of heterosexual persons to hold hands with their same-sex friends in public, as an act of solidarity with their lesbian and gay sisters and brothers who are often harassed for this behavior; the establishment of a recycling co-op in an apartment building in order to reduce nonrecycled waste and ease the deadly pressure exerted on the land by the excessive waste produced by U.S. consumers; and so on. In the movement across artificially imposed boundaries of injustice, God is.

Reimaging our interpretation of the sacred is a central component of taking seriously alternative expressions of reality as holy resource for theo-ethical praxis. Consciousness of diverse manifestations of sacred being has consistently arisen throughout Christian history. Movements that have embodied this awareness have been either marginalized or denounced as heretical in dominating white, masculinist, Western thought. The Cathars were declared heretical in the twelfth century, in part because they insisted upon a concept of two opposing divine principles. Medieval women who claimed the authority to heal, preach, and generally to act on behalf of their families and communities without ecclesial permission were burned as witches. The Shakers were dismissed from serious consideration, in part because they believe that the Second Coming must be female to bring to fullness the reality of God.

To suggest envisioning sacred presence in terms of articulation, particularly articulation through the lives of those who at best have been considered the recipients of missionary efforts by those with the power and "authority" to represent the holy, is a potentially heretical (revolutionary) act. To insist that this articulation, which embodies the holy in its very engagement with other articulate beings, is plural and multiple challenges the adequacy and efficacy of rigid monotheism as a theological reality. Given the inequitable power relationships that exist among groups in today's global context, movement toward the embodiment of sacred power — in and among those groups — necessarily implies movement into authentic solidarity through coalition. The point of coalition work, as with ecumenism and interfaith dialogue, is not to come to some ultimate unity. Rather, coalition work seeks to define the current relationships that already exist between the parties, including relationships of domination and inequality, and to move toward transformation of those areas of injustice into authentic connection. This challenge lies at the heart of the contemporary theo-ethical enterprise.

In the course of writing this book, I have lost and regained my own voice countless times, and I have undoubtedly silenced others. I have come to know more clearly the limitations *and* possibilities of a written document to adequately express complex knowings. Human voices have been the focus of my discussion, yet the voices of the earth and its other-than-human components must also be brought into any justice-centered, incarnational theo-ethic. How do we hear and echo nonhuman voices, rather than objectify them and attempt representation through the act of ventriloquism? This is a question for another time.

A theological metaphor of a static and unitary Word cannot incorporate the voices of God that echo in the lives of diverse beings and the earth on which they live. The written text, and its successor, electronic data storage, will contribute to voicing God in the world to the extent that those who generate such texts understand their voices to be but one expression of revelation. In the midst of the day-to-day lives of multiple communities and individuals, and especially in their relationships with one another, God is voiced through struggle and celebration, self-defense and education, spirited worship and birthing a baby, writing poetry and planting maize. As these many voices of justice — echoes of God — come into increasing dialogue with each other, possibilities are enhanced for the coming of the kin-dom, now and forever.

Notes

Introduction

1. Audre Lorde, "The Transformation of Silence into Language and Action," in *Sister Outsider* (Trumansburg, N.Y.: Crossing Press, 1984), 41.

2. Ibid., 44.

3. Ibid., 41.

4. Throughout this book, I use the term "theo-ethical." Use of the word "theology" — with its etymological linking of "Theos/God" with "Logos/Word" — would create a serious contradiction in my argument that the metaphor of "Word" does not serve well an enterprise that seeks to explore the presence of the sacred in multiple and diverse expressions. "Theo-ethics," on the other hand, suggests that action — or more adequately, praxis — is that which determines the extent to which the divine is embodied within the life of any community. As Enrique Dussel points out, all so-called theological reflection has its roots in fundamental ethical options. Indeed, according to Dussel, ethics is "the first kind of theology" (Enrique Dussel, *Ethics and the Theology of Liberation* [Maryknoll, N.Y.: Orbis Books, 1978], xii).

5. The patterns of thought to which I refer are developed and handed down by those who have controlled access to the political, economic, and other social institutions that have dominated Western cultures. I use the term "masculinist" (i.e., not "masculine") for two reasons. First, it is important to recognize both that some women can and do appropriate many of the characteristics of this thought and also that some men can and do resist adopting these patterns. Second, use of terms such as "masculine" and "feminine" tends toward essentialist assumptions of particular traits and characteristic ways of being inhering particularly in male or female persons.

6. See Donna Haraway, "Reading Buchi Emecheta: Contests for 'Women's Experience' in Women's Studies," in *Simians, Cyborgs, and Women: The Reinvention of Nature* (New York: Routledge, 1991), 109–24, for a discussion of the concept of "stakes" and the difference one's stakes make in the reading of a text.

7. While I privilege the works of such persons, I do not give ultimate and uncritical privilege to the *contents* of their works. Rather, I suggest an "affir-

mative action" stance in which diverse voices are engaged critically. Failure to take such voices seriously enough to disagree is yet another form of tokenistic racism. Because of the centrality of critical engagement and dialogue, the *metaphor* of voices also occupies a privileged place in this study.

8. This silence is literal and/or metaphoric. Some individuals and communities are literally silenced by a total exclusion from participation in theo-ethical dialogue. Others are metaphorically silenced through the imposition of a language not of their own choosing, a language that is inadequate to express fully their experiences.

9. Emilie M. Townes, Response to "Appropriation and Reciprocity in Womanist/Mujerista/Feminist Work," *Journal of Feminist Studies in Religion* 8, no. 2 (1992): 114–20.

Chapter 1: Power in Language

1. Pamela J. Milne, "Women and Words: The Use of Non-sexist, Inclusive Language in the Academy," *Sciences Religieuses* 18, no. 1 (1989): 27.

2. Robin Lakoff, *Language and Woman's Place* (New York: Harper Colophon, 1975).

3. Casey Miller and Kate Swift, *Words and Women: New Language in New Times* (Garden City, N.Y.: Anchor Books, 1977).

4. Dale Spender, *Man Made Language,* 2d ed. (Boston: Routledge and Kegan Paul, 1985).

5. Mary Daly, *Beyond God the Father: Toward a Philosophy of Women's Liberation* (Boston: Beacon Press, 1973). See also Mary Daly, in collaboration with Jane Caputi, *Webster's First New Intergalactic Wickedary of the English Language* (Boston: Beacon Press, 1987).

6. See, for example, Deborah Cameron, ed., *The Feminist Critique of Language: A Reader* (New York: Routledge, 1990); and Sara Mills et al., *Feminist Readings/Feminists Reading* (Charlottesville: Univ. Press of Virginia, 1989).

7. With others, I use the term "linguistic sexism," rather than the more common "sexist language," to emphasize the pervasiveness of sexist patterns throughout language constructions, and not merely in choice of individual words.

8. Letty Russell, "Inclusive Language and Power," *Religious Education* 80, no. 4 (1985): 585.

9. The age of electronic communications is challenging the adequacy of print from another direction, where discourse is dependent on the acquisition of high-technology skills and instruments. This development is at least as ambiguous as is print and has the potential to lead to still more exclusionary communication patterns in a world in which resources are inequitably distributed.

10. See Carol A. Newsom, "Woman and the Discourse of Patriarchal Wis-

dom: A Study of Proverbs 1–9," in *Gender and Difference in Ancient Israel,* ed. Peggy L. Day (Minneapolis: Fortress Press, 1989), 143.

11. I use this term as it is developed by Michel Foucault in *Power/Knowledge: Selected Interviews and Other Writings, 1972–1977,* ed. Colin Gordon (New York: Pantheon Books, 1980).

12. Sharon D. Welch, *Communities of Resistance and Solidarity: A Feminist Theology of Liberation* (Maryknoll, N.Y.: Orbis Books, 1985), 19.

13. Daly, *Webster's First New Intergalactic Wickedary,* 16. Mary Daly's contribution to the process of creative feminist reappropriation of language, and the construction of "new" words to express women's experiences, cannot be overestimated.

14. Tom F. Driver, *Patterns of Grace: Human Experience as Word of God* (San Francisco: Harper and Row, 1977), 164.

15. Ibid., 130.

16. Nelle Morton, *The Journey Is Home* (Boston: Beacon Press, 1985), 127–28; emphasis added.

17. Spender, *Man Made Language,* 123.

18. See Lakoff, *Language and Woman's Place,* and Miller and Swift, *Words and Women,* for further discussion of the incidence of tag questions in women's speech. Mary Field Belenky et al. (*Women's Ways of Knowing: The Development of Self, Voice, and Mind* [New York: Basic Books, 1986]) attribute the increased use of questioning in general in women's speech patterns to a desire to understand and respect the experience of the other(s). While acknowledging that the tentativeness implicit in ending a statement with a question makes it difficult for women's statements to be taken as seriously as those made more definitively by their brothers, Patricia Spacks suggests that "the mode of indirection and qualification allows for richer inclusiveness" (Patricia Spacks, "The Difference It Makes," in *A Feminist Perspective in the Academy: The Difference It Makes,* ed. Elizabeth Langland and Walter Gove [Chicago: Univ. of Chicago Press, 1981], 14).

19. See Gerda Lerner, *The Creation of Patriarchy* (New York: Oxford Univ. Press, 1986), for further discussion of the "man-made" qualities of language and other cultural constructions.

20. Cameron, *Feminist Critique of Language,* 150.

21. Minnie Bruce Pratt, "Identity: Skin Blood Heart," in *Yours in Struggle: Three Feminist Perspectives on Anti-Semitism and Racism,* Elly Bulkin, Minnie Bruce Pratt, and Barbara Smith (New York: Long Haul Press, 1984), 13.

22. For a variety of feminist critiques of the limitations of such a postmodernist perspective, see Linda J. Nicholson, ed., *Feminism/Postmodernism* (New York and London: Routledge, 1990).

23. Virginia Harris and Trinity Ordoña, "Developing Unity among Women of Color: Crossing the Barriers of Internalized Racism and Cross-racial Hostility," in *Making Face, Making Soul: Hacienda Caras: Creative and Critical Perspectives by Women of Color,* ed. Gloria Anzaldúa (San Francisco: Aunt Lute Foundation, 1990), 309.

24. If I am able to exercise this power in truly "comparable ways," I shall be satisfied. I am grateful beyond words to the faculty and students of Union Theological Seminary in general, and to my dissertation committee in particular, for the high degree of *em*powerment I have received in the process of pursuing my degree. We are all limited by the institutions in which we live and work, and those who encourage us to push the edges of those limits challenge the hegemony of hierarchical power.

25. The criteria I develop here emerge from my own particular context as a white feminist theo-ethicist attempting to discern some methodological insights into engaging with integrity materials emanating from communities of women whose socially sanctioned power has been more severely curtailed than has my own.

26. Judith Plaskow, "Appropriation, Reciprocity, and Issues of Power," *Journal of Feminist Studies in Religion* 8, no. 2 (1992): 108.

27. María Lugones, "On the Logic of Pluralist Feminism," in *Feminist Ethics,* ed. Claudia Card (Lawrence: Univ. Press of Kansas, 1991), 38.

28. Ibid., 41. See also Elizabeth Spelman, *Inessential Woman: Problems of Exclusion in Feminist Thought* (Boston: Beacon Press, 1988).

29. Toinette M. Eugene, "On 'Difference' and the Dream of Pluralist Feminism," *Journal of Feminist Studies in Religion* 8, no. 2 (1992): 96.

30. Trinh T. Minh-Ha, *Woman, Native, Other* (Bloomington: Univ. of Indiana, 1989), 88.

31. Sandra Harding, *Whose Science? Whose Knowledge? Thinking from Women's Lives* (Ithaca, N.Y.: Cornell Univ. Press, 1991), 246.

32. Kwok Pui-Lan, comments to a course entitled "Issues in Feminist/ Womanist Theologies," Union Theological Seminary, October 8, 1991.

33. For further discussion of the multiple possible meanings of "suffer," particularly in terms of "to bear up" with compassion, see Margaret C. Huff, *Feminist Pastoral Counseling* (Nashville: Abingdon, forthcoming), chap. 6.

34. Carter Heyward, *The Redemption of God: A Theology of Mutual Relation* (Lanham, Md.: Univ. Press of America, 1982), 221.

35. Audre Lorde, "Uses of Anger: Women Responding to Racism," in *Sister Outsider* (Trumansburg, N.Y.: Crossing Press, 1984), 127.

36. Beverly Harrison, "The Power of Anger in the Work of Love," in *Making the Connections: Essays in Feminist Social Ethics* (Boston: Beacon Press, 1985), 14.

37. Judit Moschkovich, "...But I Know You, American Woman," in *This Bridge Called My Back: Writings by Radical Women of Color,* ed. Cherríe Moraga and Gloria Anzaldúa (New York: Kitchen Table/Women of Color Press, 1981), 79. For further discussion of the imperialistic demands from white women to women of color to take responsibility for their education, see also Audre Lorde's "Age, Race, Class, and Sex: Women Defining Difference," in *Sister Outsider,* 114–23, and bell hooks's *Feminist Theory: From Margin to Center* (Boston: South End Press, 1984).

38. Pratt, "Identity," 40.

39. Lynn Andrews's *Medicine Woman* (San Francisco: Harper and Row, 1981) series is one of the most blatant examples of such misappropriation. The wide popularity of the books is testimony to the enchantment of white, Euro-American women with anything that has the potential to fill the spiritual emptiness they experience in denying their own ethnic and cultural roots.

40. Kwok Pui-Lan, "Speaking from the Margins," *Journal of Feminist Studies in Religion* 8, no. 2 (1992): 103.

41. Patricia Hill Collins, *Black Feminist Thought: Knowledge, Consciousness, and the Politics of Empowerment* (Boston: Unwin Hyman, 1990), 225.

42. Susan Thistlethwaite, *Sex, Race, and God: Christian Feminism in Black and White* (New York: Crossroad, 1989), 25.

43. For a discussion of the concept of freely chosen "traitorous locations," which challenge the norms of a hegemonic culture, see Sandra Harding, *Whose Science?* 268–95.

44. Lynet Uttal, "Inclusion without Influence: The Continuing Tokenism of Women of Color," in *Making Face, Making Soul,* 42–43.

45. Ada María Isasi-Díaz, "Viva la Diferencia!" *Journal of Feminist Studies in Religion* 8, no. 2 (1992): 101.

46. Beverly Harrison, "Theological Reflection in the Struggle for Liberation: A Feminist Perspective," in *Making the Connections,* 244.

Chapter 2: And the Word Was Made Man

1. Carter Heyward, "An Unfinished Symphony of Liberation: The Radicalization of Christian Feminism among White U.S. Women," *Journal of Feminist Studies in Religion* 1, no. 1 (Spring 1985): 118.

2. Excerpted from Maya Angelou, "On the Pulse of Morning," poem commissioned for and read by the poet at the inauguration of President William Jefferson Clinton (New York: Random House, 1993).

3. Donna Haraway, "A Cyborg Manifesto: Science, Technology, and Socialist-Feminism in the Late Twentieth Century," in *Simians, Cyborgs, and Women: The Reinvention of Nature* (New York: Routledge, 1991), 154.

4. Cherríe Moraga, "Amar en los Años de Guerra," in *Loving in the War Years* (Boston: South End Press, 1983), viii. Translation: "The death of my grandmother. And I never spoke to her in the language she could understand."

5. Ursula Le Guin, "Bryn Mawr Commencement Address (1986)," in *Dancing at the Edge of the World* (New York: Grove Press, 1989), 160.

6. For a helpful outline of the sequential development of usage of the concept of "Word" in Christian history, see Frederick E. Crowe, *Theology of the Christian Word: A Study in History* (New York: Paulist Press, 1978).

7. For an exploration of some of the earliest understandings of "Logos" in Greek thought, see F. E. Walton, *Development of the Logos Doctrine in Greek and Hebrew Thought* (London: Limpkin, Marshall, Hamilton, Kent, 1911).

8. Andrea Nye, *Words of Power: A Feminist Reading of the History of Logic* (New York: Routledge, 1990), 23.

9. Ibid., 23.

10. Ibid., 25–28.

11. Ibid., 32.

12. Ibid., 37.

13. Ibid., 41.

14. Ibid., 49.

15. Ibid., 57.

16. Ibid., 67.

17. Ibid., 77.

18. Ibid., 79.

19. Ibid.

20. Hans Schwarz, *Divine Communication: Word and Sacrament in Biblical, Historical, and Contemporary Perspective* (Philadelphia: Fortress Press, 1985), 9–10.

21. Walter J. Ong, *The Presence of the Word: Some Prolegomena for Cultural and Religious History* (New Haven, Conn.: Yale Univ. Press, 1967), 12.

22. Ibid., 14. See also Judith Plaskow, *Standing again at Sinai: Judaism from a Feminist Perspective* (San Francisco: Harper and Row, 1990), for elaboration of the open-ended and dynamic qualities of Torah in Judaism.

23. Ong, *Presence of the Word*, 12.

24. Ibid., 22.

25. Ibid.; emphasis added.

26. Ibid., 54.

27. Ibid., 63.

28. Ibid., 78.

29. Ibid., 65. See also Casey Miller and Kate Swift, *Words and Women: New Language in New Times* (Garden City, N.Y.: Anchor Books, 1977), 84ff., for a discussion of grammarians' attempts to control English by acts of Parliament and Congress, and Deborah Cameron, ed., *The Feminist Critique of Language: A Reader* (New York: Routledge, 1990), 150, for discussion of the "socio-political aspects of dictionary-making."

30. Writing in 1967, in the euphoria generated amidst liberal Catholics by Vatican II, Ong may have had more cause for optimism than is possible in the reactionary climate of the 1990s. Neither did Ong recognize the plurality of voices that is central to this study.

31. Dorothee Sölle, *Beyond Mere Obedience* (New York: Pilgrim Press, 1982), 8.

32. Ibid., 25.

33. See Stanley B. Marrow, *The Words of Jesus in Our Gospels: A Catholic Response to Fundamentalism* (New York: Paulist Press, 1979).

34. Kathleen B. Jones, *Compassionate Authority: Democracy and the Representation of Women* (New York: Routledge, 1993).

35. Ibid., 21.

36. Ibid., 34.

37. Ibid., 40.

38. Delores S. Williams, *Sisters in the Wilderness: The Challenge of Womanist God-talk* (Maryknoll, N.Y.: Orbis Books, 1993), 188. See also Renita Weems, *Just a Sister Away: A Womanist Vision of Women's Relationships in the Bible* (San Diego: Lura Media, 1988), and Elsa Tamez, ed., *Through Her Eyes: Women's Theology from Latin America* (Maryknoll, N.Y.: Orbis Books, 1989), for other examples of the creative appropriation of biblical material in women's survival struggles.

39. Claudia Camp, "Female Voice, Written Word: Women and Authority in Hebrew Scripture," in *Embodied Love: Sensuality and Relationship as Feminist Values*, ed. Paula M. Cooey, Sharon A. Farmer, and Mary Ellen Ross (San Francisco: Harper and Row, 1987), 98. See also Letty Russell, *Household of Freedom: Authority in Feminist Theology* (Philadelphia, Westminster Press, 1987).

40. Tom F. Driver, *Christ in a Changing World: Toward an Ethical Christology* (New York: Crossroad, 1981), 86.

41. Ibid., 90.

42. Ong, *Presence of the Word*, 14.

43. Ibid., 268.

44. Frederick E. Greenspahn, introduction to *Scripture in the Jewish and Christian Traditions: Authority, Interpretation, Relevance*, ed. Frederick E. Greenspahn (Nashville: Abingdon Press, 1982), 11.

45. Marrow, *Words of Jesus*, 26. See Letty Russell, "Inclusive Language and Power," *Religious Education* 80, no. 4 (1985): 582–602, for a more adequate assessment of the "ascending" perspective mentioned by Marrow.

46. Marrow, *Words of Jesus*, 30.

47. Sallie McFague, *Metaphorical Theology: Models of God in Religious Language* (Philadelphia: Fortress Press, 1982), 4.

48. Williams, *Sisters in the Wilderness*, 188.

49. Elisabeth Schüssler Fiorenza, *Bread Not Stone: The Challenge of Feminist Biblical Interpretation* (Boston: Beacon Press, 1984), 146.

50. Elisabeth Schüssler Fiorenza, *But She Said: Feminist Practices of Biblical Interpretation* (Boston: Beacon Press, 1992), 35.

51. Ibid., 42.

52. Ibid., 76.

53. See James Cone, *The Spirituals and the Blues* (New York: Seabury Press, 1972), for an exemplary account of the ways in which reinterpretation of biblical themes served as empowerment for survival and liberation for enslaved peoples.

54. Schüssler Fiorenza, *But She Said*, 132.

55. Juan Donoso Cortés, *An Essay on Catholicism, Authority and Order Considered in Their Fundamental Principles* (Westport, Conn.: Hyperion Press, 1925), 70.

56. Rosemary Radford Ruether, "Differing Views of the Church," in *Authority, Community, and Conflict,* ed. Madonna Kolbenschlag (Kansas City: Sheed and Ward, 1986), 97.

57. Daniel C. Maguire, "Accountability of Leaders," in *A Catholic Bill of Rights,* ed. Leonard Swidler and Herbert O'Brien (Kansas City: Sheed and Ward, 1988), 52.

58. Adrian Hastings, "Catholic History from Vatican I to John Paul II," in *Modern Catholicism: Vatican II and After,* ed. A. Hastings (New York: Oxford Univ. Press, 1991), 2.

59. Ibid., 1.

60. Monika K. Hellwig, "A Theological Perspective," in *Authority, Community, and Conflict,* 134.

61. David J. O'Brien, "An Historical Perspective," in *Authority, Community, and Conflict,* 109.

62. Edmund Hill, *Ministry and Authority in the Catholic Church* (London: Geoffrey Chapman, 1988), 4; emphasis added.

63. For a critical analysis of differing perceptions of "church," see Leonardo Boff, *Church: Charism and Power: Liberation Theology and the Institutional Church* (New York: Crossroad, 1985). See also Avery Dulles, *Models of the Church* (Garden City, N.Y.: Doubleday, 1978).

64. Alicia Suskin Ostriker, *Stealing the Language: The Emergence of Women's Poetry in America* (Boston: Beacon Press, 1986), 161.

65. Driver, *Christ in a Changing World,* 18.

66. Nelle Morton, "Preaching the Word," in *Sexist Religion and Women in the Church,* ed. Alice Hageman (New York: Association Press, 1974), 39.

67. Rebecca Chopp's *The Power to Speak: Feminism, Language, God* (New York: Crossroad, 1989), while addressing the issue of language and God, attempts to reclaim the metaphor of Word in ways too abstract to be helpful in my current project. Standing firmly in the tradition of much contemporary postmodern thought, Chopp's exposition fails either to give voice to multiple perspectives or to provide a theo-ethical or political methodology for doing so.

68. Rosemary Radford Ruether, *Sexism and God-talk: Toward a Feminist Theology* (Boston: Beacon Press, 1983), 58.

69. Susan Cady, Marian Ronan, and Hal Taussig, *Sophia: The Future of Feminist Spirituality* (San Francisco: Harper and Row, 1986), 67–68.

70. Schüssler Fiorenza, *But She Said,* 13. See also Elizabeth Johnson, *She Who Is: The Mystery of God in Feminist Theological Discourse* (New York: Crossroad, 1992), 124–87, for an extended discussion of Sophia as Spirit, Jesus, and Mother.

71. Cady, Ronan, and Taussig, *Sophia,* 24.

72. Ibid., 44.

73. Ibid., 36–37.

74. Elisabeth Schüssler Fiorenza, *In Memory of Her: A Feminist Theological Reconstruction of Christian Origins* (Boston: Beacon Press, 1984), 132.

75. Cady, Ronan, and Taussig, *Sophia,* 41.

76. Ibid., 84–85.

77. See particularly Irenaeus of Lyons's identification of Logos and Wisdom as Son and Spirit, the two hands of God. Irenaeus of Lyons, *Against the Heresies,* trans. A. Roberts and W. H. Rambaut (Edinburgh: T. and T. Clark, 1869), 5.6.

78. Sharon D. Welch, *A Feminist Ethic of Risk* (Philadelphia: Fortress Press, 1990).

79. Ibid., 1–47.

80. Ibid., 127.

81. Ibid., 19.

82. Ibid., 168.

83. Ibid.

84. Ibid., 2.

85. Ibid., 139.

86. Ibid., 15.

87. See the special section, "Appropriation and Reciprocity in Womanist/ Mujerista/Feminist Work," *Journal of Feminist Studies in Religion* 8, no. 2 (Fall 1992): 91–122, with articles by Toinette Eugene, Ada María Isasi-Díaz, Kwok Pui-Lan, Judith Plaskow, Mary Hunt, Emilie Townes, and Ellen Umansky, for a multicultural discussion of the issues involved in the use of one another's work.

88. Welch, *Feminist Ethic of Risk,* 136.

89. Ibid., 168.

90. Ibid., 111.

91. Ibid., 173.

92. Ibid., 178.

93. bell hooks, *Talking Back: Thinking Feminist, Thinking Black* (Boston: South End Press, 1989), 37.

94. Patricia Hill Collins, *Black Feminist Thought: Knowledge, Consciousness, and the Politics of Empowerment* (Boston: Unwin Hyman, 1990), 15.

95. Susan Thistlethwaite, *Sex, Race, and God: Christian Feminism in Black and White* (New York: Crossroad, 1989).

96. Ibid., 12.

97. Ibid., 27–43, 86.

98. Beverly Harrison, "The Power of Anger in the Work of Love: Christian Ethics for Women and Other Strangers," in *Making the Connections,* ed. Carol Robb (Boston: Beacon Press, 1985), 16.

99. Delores S. Williams, "Womanist Theology: Black Women's Voices," in *Yearning to Breathe Free: Liberation Theologies in the U.S.,* ed. Mar Peter-Raoul, Linda Forcey, and Robert Hunter (Maryknoll, N.Y.: Orbis Books, 1990), 66.

100. Thistlethwaite, *Sex, Race, and God,* 87.

101. Ibid., 22–24.

102. Ibid., 46.

Chapter 3: Voices of the Kin-Dom of God

1. The term "kin-dom of God" is used by Ada María Isasi-Díaz and Yolanda Tarango, *Hispanic Women: Prophetic Voice in the Church* (San Francisco: Harper and Row, 1988), xvii, to denote a community of mutuality and equality rather than a monarchical being ruling "his" subject people.

2. The term "authorship" is used here in its more inclusive sense of "the state or act of writing, creating, or causing," rather than its limited application to writing alone.

3. Rigoberta Menchú, *I, Rigoberta Menchú: An Indian Woman in Guatemala*, ed. Elisabeth Burgos-Debray; trans. Ann Wright (London: Verso, 1984), 59.

4. Menchú and others are by no means naive about the powers marshaled against them. Delores S. Williams, *Sisters in the Wilderness: The Challenge of Womanist God-talk* (Maryknoll, N.Y.: Orbis Books, 1993), develops a helpful understanding of "strength" that suggests parallels with what I am calling agency. Williams's interpretation enables a clear distinction between the strength/agency demonstrated by Menchú and African-American slave women, for example, and the power exerted by the Guatemalan government and southern U.S. plantation owners.

5. Jarena Lee, "The Life and Religious Experience of Jarena Lee, a Coloured Lady, Giving an Account of Her Call to Preach the Gospel," in *Sisters of the Spirit: Three Black Women's Autobiographies of the Nineteenth Century*, ed. William L. Andrews (Bloomington: Indiana Univ. Press, 1986), 36.

6. Zilpha Elaw, "Memoirs of the Life, Religious Experience, Ministerial Travels and Labours of Mrs. Zilpha Elaw, an American Female of Colour; Together with Some Account of the Great Religious Revivals in America [Written by Herself]," in *Sisters of the Spirit*, 124.

7. Ibid., 147.

8. Julia A. J. Foote, "A Brand Plucked from the Fire: An Autobiographical Sketch," in *Sisters of the Spirit*, 170.

9. Ibid., 209.

10. Onnie Lee Logan, *Motherwit: An Alabama Midwife's Story*, in collaboration with Kathryn Clark (New York: E. P. Hutton, 1989), 90; emphasis added.

11. Ibid., ix–x.

12. Ibid., 142.

13. Kathleen Hirsch, *Songs from the Alley* (New York: Doubleday, 1989).

14. Ibid., 230.

15. Ibid., 235.

16. Ibid., 261.

17. Ibid., 264.

18. Suzette Haden Elgin, "Women's Language and Near Future Science Fiction: A Reply," *Women's Studies* 14 (1987): 178.

19. Suzette Haden Elgin, *Native Tongue* (New York: Daw Books, 1984); idem, *Native Tongue II: The Judas Rose* (New York: Daw Books, 1987); and idem, *Native Tongue III: Earthsong* (New York: Daw Books, 1994).

20. Elgin, "Women's Language," 179. See also idem, *A First Dictionary and Grammar of Láadan,* ed. Diane Martin (Madison, Wis.: Society for the Furtherance and Study of Fantasy and Science Fiction, 1988). A network has developed of persons who continue to work on the expansion of Láadan.

21. I am grateful to Delores Williams for this term that underlies Williams's own insistence on the existence of multiple effective resistance strategies within the black community's history.

22. Elgin, *Native Tongue,* 22.

23. Elgin, *A First Dictionary,* 93.

24. Ibid., 267.

25. Jeannette Armstrong, "Words," in *Telling It: Women and Language across Cultures,* ed. Telling It Book Collective (Vancouver: Press Gang Publishers, 1990), 24.

26. Ibid., 25–26.

27. Ibid., 28.

28. Paula Gunn Allen, *The Sacred Hoop: Recovering the Feminine in American Indian Traditions* (Boston: Beacon Press, 1986), 55.

29. See especially the works of James Weldon Johnson, James Baldwin, Ralph Ellison, Zora Neale Hurston, and Alice Walker.

30. Geneva Smitherman, "Black Language as Power," in *Language and Power,* ed. Cheris Kramarae, Muriel Schulz, and William O'Barr (Beverly Hills, Calif.: Sage Publications, 1984), 110.

31. Ibid., 115.

32. Ibid., 104–5.

33. Ibid., 106.

34. June Jordan, "Nobody Mean More to Me Than You and the Future Life of Willie Jordan," in *On Call: Political Essays* (Boston: South End Press, 1985), 123.

35. Katie G. Cannon, *Black Womanist Ethics* (Atlanta, Ga.: Scholars Press, 1988), 78.

36. Ibid., 85.

37. Ibid., 90; emphasis added.

38. Logan, *Motherwit,* 65.

39. Ibid., 59.

40. Marjorie Bard, *Shadow Women: Homeless Women's Survival Stories* (Kansas City: Sheed and Ward, 1990), 93.

41. Menchú, *I, Rigoberta Menchú,* 41.

42. Ibid., 119, 120–21.

43. Ibid., 166.

44. Renny Golden, *The Hour of the Poor, the Hour of Women: Salvadoran Women Speak* (New York: Crossroad, 1991), 102.

45. Menchú, *I, Rigoberta Menchú,* 180.

46. Ibid., 196.

47. Octavia E. Butler, interview in Larry McCaffery, *Across the Wounded Galaxies: Interviews with Contemporary Science Fiction Writers* (Urbana: Univ. of Illinois Press, 1990), 63–64.

48. Octavia E. Butler, *Wild Seed* (New York: Pocket Books, 1980), and idem, *Kindred* (Boston: Beacon Press, 1988). The refusal of easy resolution to difficult issues is characteristic of much feminist SF. See also Ursula K. Le Guin, *The Dispossessed* (New York: Harper and Row, 1974); Marti Steussy, *Forest of the Night* (New York: Ballantine Books, 1987); Anne McCaffery, *Decision at Doona* (New York: Ballantine Books, 1969).

49. Elgin, *Native Tongue II*, 231.

50. Lee Maracle, "Ramparts Hanging in the Air," in *Telling It*, 171.

51. Menchú, *I, Rigoberta Menchú*, 84.

52. Williams, *Sisters in the Wilderness*, passim.

53. The FMLN was founded in 1980 as a united front of five resistance guerrilla armies.

54. Golden, *Hour of the Poor*, 174.

55. Ibid., 178.

56. Menchú, *I, Rigoberta Menchú*, 130.

57. Ibid., 131–32.

58. Ibid., 134–35.

59. Melanie Kaye/Kantrowitz, *The Issue Is Power: Essays on Women, Jews, Violence and Resistance* (San Francisco: Aunt Lute Books, 1992), 64.

60. Menchú, *I, Rigoberta Menchú*, 13.

61. Ibid., 19.

62. Ibid., 56.

63. Ibid., 133–34.

64. Ibid., 134.

65. Ibid., 125.

66. Golden, *Hour of the Poor*, 57.

67. Ibid., 98.

68. Logan, *Motherwit*, 177.

69. Joy Kogawa, "From the Bottom of the Well, from the Distant Stars," in *Telling It*, 96–97.

70. Chung Hyun Kyung, *Struggle to Be the Sun Again: Introducing Asian Women's Theology* (Maryknoll, N.Y.: Orbis Books, 1990), 49.

71. María Clara Bingemer, "Reflections on the Trinity," in *Through Her Eyes: Women's Theology from Latin America*, ed. Elsa Tamez (Maryknoll, N.Y.: Orbis Books, 1989), 61.

72. Menchú, *I, Rigoberta Menchú*, 8.

73. Ibid., 15.

74. Ibid., 55.

75. Golden, *Hour of the Poor*, 65.

76. Ibid.

77. Logan, *Motherwit*, 43.

78. Menchú, *I, Rigoberta Menchú*, 65.
79. Ibid., 133.
80. Ibid., 204.
81. Golden, *Hour of the Poor*, 73.
82. Williams, *Sisters in the Wilderness*, 6.
83. Allen, *Sacred Hoop*, 160.
84. Golden, *Hour of the Poor*, 192, 193.
85. Allen, *Sacred Hoop*, 267.

Chapter 4: Boundaries of Knowledge, Barriers to Knowing

1. Carol Gilligan, *In a Different Voice: Psychological Theory and Women's Development* (Cambridge, Mass.: Harvard Univ. Press, 1982).
2. Mary Belenky et al., *Women's Ways of Knowing: The Development of Self, Voice, and Mind* (New York: Basic Books, 1986).
3. See Judith Jordan et al., *Women's Growth in Connection: Writings from the Stone Center* (New York: Guilford Press, 1991). This book contains selected "working papers" from the series published by the Stone Center.
4. Belenky et al., *Women's Ways of Knowing*, insist that their schema should not be viewed as a stage theory, yet I find it impossible to read the text without valuing constructive knowing over the other "ways" presented and detecting a sense of progressive movement through at least some of the other modes toward this ideal.
5. Ibid., 51.
6. In advocating this "way of knowing," I acknowledge also the multiple social forces which inhibit women's achievement and expression of constructivist knowing. What I suggest here is that such a mode of knowing provides a model of authority and agency worth striving for.
7. Belenky et al., *Women's Ways of Knowing*, 152.
8. Onnie Lee Logan, *Motherwit: An Alabama Midwife's Story*, in collaboration with Kathryn Clark (New York: E. P. Hutton, 1989), passim.
9. When I propose the incorporation of creativity into the academy, I am not promoting an anti-intellectual approach that devalues reading and writing. Rather, I seek to challenge the exclusivity of those forms of expression and information-gathering in most academic settings and suggest that diverse creative enterprises can be incorporated without any loss of academic integrity — indeed, that they *must* be incorporated if educational systems are to *achieve* integrity.
10. Elizabeth Minnick calls this hierarchical ranking of knowledge forms "hierarchically invidious monism." Minnick explains the system in which this monism evolves as one in which "one category is taken to be not literally all there is, but the highest, most significant, most valuable, and, critically, most real category" (Elizabeth Minnick, *Transforming Knowledge* [Philadelphia: Temple Univ. Press, 1990], 53).

11. See Kathleen B. Jones, "The Trouble with Authority," *Differences: A Journal of Feminist Cultural Studies* 3, no. 1 (1991): 109. See also idem, *Compassionate Authority: Democracy and the Representation of Women* (New York: Routledge, 1993).

12. Minnick, *Transforming Knowledge,* 151–52.

13. Ibid., 171.

14. Ibid., 172.

15. Donna Haraway, "A Cyborg Manifesto: Science, Technology, and Socialist-Feminism in the Late Twentieth Century," in *Simians, Cyborgs, and Women: The Reinvention of Nature* (New York: Routledge, 1991), 149–82.

16. *Webster's Ninth New Collegiate Dictionary;* emphasis added.

17. Haraway, "A Cyborg Manifesto," 150.

18. Ibid., 151–53.

19. Ibid., 150.

20. Patricia Hill Collins, *Black Feminist Thought: Knowledge, Consciousness, and the Politics of Empowerment* (Boston: Unwin Hyman, 1990), 15.

21. See bell hooks and Cornel West, *Breaking Bread: Insurgent Black Intellectual Life* (Boston: South End Press, 1991), especially chap. 3, for a further discussion of this distinction.

22. The term "the practice of freedom," employed in the subheading for this section, is used by Paulo Freire in his *Pedagogy of the Oppressed* (New York: Continuum, 1970).

23. Logan, *Motherwit,* ix–x.

24. bell hooks, *Talking Back: Thinking Feminist, Thinking Black* (Boston: South End Press, 1989), 105–11.

25. Shane Phelan, *Identity Politics: Lesbian Feminism and the Limits of Community* (Philadelphia: Temple Univ. Press, 1989), 49.

26. Collins, *Black Feminist Thought,* 32; emphasis added.

27. Donna Haraway, "Reading Buchi Emecheta: Contests for 'Women's Experience' in Women's Studies," in *Simians, Cyborgs, and Women,* 114.

28. Rigoberta Menchú, *I, Rigoberta Menchú: An Indian Woman in Guatemala,* ed. Elisabeth Burgos-Debray; trans. Ann Wright (London: Verso, 1984).

29. Collins, *Black Feminist Thought,* 209.

30. Ada María Isasi-Díaz and Yolanda Tarango, *Hispanic Women: Prophetic Voice in the Church* (San Francisco: Harper and Row, 1988), 50–51.

31. Ibid., 79.

32. Audre Lorde, "Poetry Is Not a Luxury," in *Sister Outsider* (Trumansburg, N.Y.: Crossing Press, 1984), 37.

33. Judy Grahn, "The Common Woman," in *The Work of a Common Woman,* introduction by Adrienne Rich (New York: St. Martin's Press, 1978), 73.

34. Chung Hyun Kyung, *Struggle to Be the Sun Again: Introducing Asian Women's Theology* (Maryknoll, N.Y.: Orbis Books, 1990), 104.

35. Ibid., 3.

36. Carter Heyward, *Touching Our Strength: The Erotic as Power and the Love of God* (San Francisco: Harper and Row, 1989), 93; emphasis added.

37. Cherríe Moraga, *Loving in the War Years* (Boston: South End Press, 1983), 133. bell hooks uses the term "yearning" to speak of a similar passionately embodied longing to engage one another across lines of difference. See hooks, *Yearning: Race, Gender, and Cultural Politics* (Boston: South End Press, 1990), 13.

38. Isasi-Díaz and Tarango, *Hispanic Women*, 106.

39. Freire, *Pedagogy of the Oppressed*, 75.

40. Isasi-Díaz and Tarango, *Hispanic Women*, 96.

41. Ibid., 98.

42. Ibid., 99.

43. See Joe Holland and Peter Henriot, *Social Analysis: Linking Faith and Justice* (Washington, D.C.: Center of Concern, 1980).

44. Isasi-Díaz and Tarango, *Hispanic Women*, 100.

45. Ibid., 102.

46. Ibid., 2.

47. Ibid., 62.

48. Mary Midgley, *Evolution as a Religion: Strange Hopes and Stranger Fears* (London and New York: Methuen, 1985), 3.

49. Ibid., 107.

50. Ibid., 112.

51. Ibid., 134.

52. I thank Anne Gilson for this story.

53. This term is used by Donna J. Haraway in *Primate Visions: Gender, Race, and Nature in the World of Modern Science* (New York: Routledge, 1989), 5. Haraway includes such other possible terms as "speculative fiction," "science fantasy," "speculative futures," and "speculative fabulation."

54. Ibid., 15.

55. Marleen Barr, *Feminist Fabulation: Space/Postmodern Fiction* (Iowa City: Univ. of Iowa Press, 1992), xiv; emphasis added.

56. Ibid., 8. See also bell hooks, *Black Looks: Race and Representation* (Boston: South End Press, 1992), 170, for a discussion of the way in which stereotypes function as "fantasy," in the sense that they are "a projection onto the Other that makes them less threatening."

57. Haraway, *Primate Visions*, 4.

58. Ursula K. Le Guin, "Why Are Americans Afraid of Dragons?" in *The Language of the Night: Essays on Fantasy and Science Fiction* (New York: HarperCollins, 1989), 39–40.

59. Ibid., 73.

60. Ursula K. Le Guin, "The Carrier Bag Theory of Fiction," in *Dancing at the Edge of the World: Thoughts on Words, Women, Places* (New York: Grove Press, 1989), 170.

61. Sallie McFague, *Metaphorical Theology: Models of God in Religious Language* (Philadelphia: Fortress Press, 1982), 163–64.

62. Marti J. Steussy, "Why I Write Science Fiction," *Encounter* 52, no. 1 (Winter 1991): 83; emphasis added.

63. Ibid., 84.

64. Ibid., 84–85.

65. Ibid., 85–86.

66. Barr, *Feminist Fabulation*, 14.

67. hooks, *Black Looks*, 50–51. Octavia Butler's SF is, I suggest, an exception to this pattern. See particularly *Wild Seed* (New York: Pocket Books, 1980).

68. Barr, *Feminist Fabulation*, 151.

69. Ursula K. Le Guin, "The Child and the Shadow," in *Language of the Night*, 65–66.

70. Ursula K. Le Guin, "Introduction to 'The Word for World Is Forest,'" in *Language of the Night*, 145.

71. Ursula K. Le Guin, "Escape Routes," in *Language of the Night*, 207.

72. Ursula K. Le Guin, "The Stone Ax and the Muskoxen," in *Language of the Night*, 222–23.

73. Haraway, *Primate Visions*, 8.

74. Menchú, *I, Rigoberta Menchú*, 122–30.

75. Bard, *Shadow Women*, 47–85.

76. See, for example, Ursula K. Le Guin, *The Left Hand of Darkness* (New York: Ace, 1969).

77. See the works of Mercedes Lackey, Elizabeth Moon, and C.J. Cherryh for examples of this specific dimension of SF.

78. Marion Zimmer Bradley's *Darkover* series is a good example of a "world" originally imagined into being by an author but continually developed by multiple others, often in collaboration with the original author and with each other.

79. Isasi-Díaz and Tarango, *Hispanic Women*, 81.

80. Chung, *Struggle to Be the Sun Again*, 39.

81. Ibid., 44–45.

82. Ibid., 101.

83. hooks, *Yearning*, 12–13.

Chapter 5: Boundaries of Identity, Barriers to Voices

1. I recognize that religious institutions such as black churches in the United States offer an alternative experience, frequently positive and affirming at least of African-American men.

2. M. Scott Peck, *The Different Drum: Community Making and Peace* (New York: Simon and Schuster, 1987).

3. Conversely, Serbian Christians "struggle" to exterminate the Bosnian Muslims, and the Guatemalan government "struggles" to eliminate the "subversives" who are attempting to ensure the survival of their people in the highlands of Quiché.

4. I stress the term "recognition" here to indicate that all theories and systems of thought have been rooted in the experiences of those developing and propagating them, regardless of claims of objectivity and lack of self-interest. In making explicit their own social location and stakes in undertaking their work, liberatory theorists illuminate also the extent to which the masking of such factors by those steeped in the white Western masculinist paradigm has silenced the voices of those who do not share in the characteristics of the dominant — and dominating — group.

5. Sweet Honey in the Rock, "Breaths," from the album *Good News* (Chicago: Flying Fish Records, 1981).

6. Cherríe Moraga, *Loving in the War Years* (Boston: South End Press, 1983), 51.

7. Audre Lorde, "Eye to Eye: Black Women, Hatred, and Anger," in *Sister Outsider* (Trumansburg, N.Y.: Crossing Press, 1984), 152.

8. bell hooks, *Yearning: Race, Gender, and Cultural Politics* (Boston: South End Press, 1990), 47.

9. Alice Walker, *In Search of Our Mothers' Gardens* (San Diego: Harcourt Brace Jovanovich, 1983), xi.

10. Bernice Johnson Reagon, "Coalition Politics: Turning the Century," in *Home Girls: A Black Feminist Anthology,* ed. Barbara Smith (New York: Kitchen Table/Women of Color Press, 1983), 361.

11. Melanie Kaye/Kantrowitz, *The Issue Is Power: Essays on Women, Jews, Violence and Resistance* (San Francisco: Aunt Lute Books, 1992), 79.

12. Ada María Isasi-Díaz and Yolanda Tarango, *Hispanic Women: Prophetic Voice in the Church* (San Francisco: Harper and Row, 1988), 78–79.

13. Katie G. Cannon, *Black Womanist Ethics* (Atlanta, Ga.: Scholars Press, 1988), 18.

14. bell hooks and Cornel West, *Breaking Bread: Insurgent Black Intellectual Life* (Boston: South End Press, 1991), 18.

15. Ibid., 93–94.

16. hooks, *Yearning,* 36; emphasis added.

17. See also hooks, *Black Looks,* 33.

18. Cannon, *Black Womanist Ethics,* 48.

19. Isasi-Díaz and Tarango, *Hispanic Women,* 105–6.

20. Audre Lorde, *Zami: A New Spelling of My Name* (Trumansburg, N.Y.: Crossing Press, 1982), 197.

21. Ibid., 226.

22. Lorde, "Age, Race, Class, and Sex," in *Sister Outsider,* 120–21. The reaction of lesbian and gay organizations to the "Don't ask, don't tell, don't pursue" compromise/capitulation of the Clinton administration in the United States regarding lesbians and gay men in the military illustrates the growing

awareness among lesbian and gay persons of the high cost of such silence and secrecy.

23. See Suzanne Pharr, *Homophobia: A Weapon of Sexism* (Inverness, Calif.: Chardon Press, 1988), for a discussion of lesbian-baiting and its effectiveness in dividing women's communities.

24. Moraga, *Loving in the War Years*, 140–41.

25. Reagon, "Coalition Politics," 367.

26. Ibid., 358.

27. Caryatis Cardea, "Lesbian Revolution and the 50 Minute Hour: A Working-class Look at Therapy and the Movement," in *Lesbian Philosophies and Cultures*, ed. Jeffner Allen (Albany: State Univ. of New York Press, 1990), 193–218.

28. hooks, *Yearning*, 28.

29. Faith Nolan, "I Black Woman," from the album *Freedom to Love* (Emeryville, Calif.: Redwood Records, 1989).

30. Collins, *Black Feminist Thought*, 170. In a helpful insight into the supposed "naturalness" of certain defined characteristics imagined to adhere to particular groups of persons, Ursula K. Le Guin defines "natural" as "happily acculturated." See Ursula K. Le Guin, *The Language of the Night: Essays on Fantasy and Science Fiction* (New York: HarperCollins, 1989), 135.

31. hooks, *Yearning*, 28–29.

32. Kaye/Kantrowitz, *The Issue Is Power*, 182.

33. Those who chose to stay within the original group may also have chosen a morally committed position, one that many of them believe demands that they continue to struggle from *within* the institutional setting.

34. Kaye/Kantrowitz, *The Issue Is Power*, 203.

35. Lorde, "The Uses of Anger," in *Sister Outsider*, 132.

36. Kaye/Kantrowitz, *The Issue Is Power*, 199.

37. Judith Butler, *Gender Trouble: Feminism and the Subversion of Identity* (New York: Routledge, 1990), 148.

38. Nancy Hartsock, "The Feminist Standpoint: Developing the Ground for a Specifically Feminist Historical Materialism," in *Discovering Reality: Feminist Perspectives on Epistemology, Metaphysics, Methodology, and Philosophy of Science*, ed. Sandra Harding and Merrill Hintikka (Dordrecht, Holland: D. Reidel, 1983), 283–310.

39. For such criticisms, see Linda Nicholson, ed., *Feminism/Postmodernism* (New York: Routledge, 1990), and Rosemary Hennessey, *Materialist Feminism and the Politics of Discourse* (New York: Routledge, 1993).

40. Hartsock, "Feminist Standpoint," 285.

41. Donna Haraway, "Situated Knowledges," in *Simians, Cyborgs, and Women: The Reinvention of Nature* (New York: Routledge, 1991), 191.

42. Sandra Harding, "Rethinking Standpoint Epistemology: 'What Is Strong Objectivity?' " in *Feminist Epistemologies*, ed. Linda Alcoff and Elizabeth Potter (New York and London: Routledge, 1993), 55.

43. Vrinda Dalmiya and Linda Alcoff, "Are 'Old Wives' Tales' Justified?" in *Feminist Epistemologies*, 241.

44. Sandra Harding, *Whose Science? Whose Knowledge? Thinking from Women's Lives* (Ithaca, N.Y.: Cornell Univ. Press, 1991), 269.

45. Toinette Eugene, "On 'Difference' and the Dream of Pluralist Feminism," *Journal of Feminist Studies in Religion* 8, no. 2 (1992): 97.

46. Donna Haraway, "Daughters of Man-the-Hunter," in *Simians, Cyborgs, and Women: The Reinvention of Nature* (New York: Routledge, 1991), 106.

47. Collins, *Black Feminist Thought*, 17. See also Hennessey, *Materialist Feminism*, 13.

48. See Harding, *Whose Science?* chap. 6, for a detailed exposition of the distinction she makes here, and particularly the relationship between "strong" objectivity and socially situated knowledge.

49. Harding, "Rethinking Standpoint Epistemology," 71.

50. Ibid.

51. Sandra Harding, "The Instability of the Analytical Categories of Feminist Theory," *Signs: Journal of Women in Culture and Society* 11, no. 4 (1986): 645–64.

52. Ibid., 649.

53. Nancie Caraway, *Segregated Sisterhood: Racism and the Politics of American Feminism* (Knoxville: Univ. of Tennessee Press, 1991), 19.

54. Ibid., 171–74. I will return to the need for "oppositional identities" in the shift into coalition for action. Here, I emphasize the choice involved in such identities.

55. hooks, *Yearning*, 131.

56. Ibid., 153.

57. bell hooks, *Feminist Theory: From Margin to Center* (Boston: South End Press, 1984), 163.

58. Harding, *Whose Science?* 284–86.

59. Collins, *Black Feminist Thought*, 21.

60. Hennessey, *Materialist Feminism*, xii.

61. Ibid., 71.

62. Ibid., 73. See also Michéle Barrett and Anne Phillips, eds., *Destabilizing Theory: Contemporary Feminist Debates* (Stanford, Calif.: Stanford Univ. Press, 1992).

63. Caraway, *Segregated Sisterhood*, 62; emphasis added.

64. Collins, *Black Feminist Thought*, 226.

65. Haraway, "Situated Knowledges," 187.

66. I am indebted to Margaret C. Huff for this phrase and for extended conversations about the possibilities inherent in ambiguity and paradox, particularly when applied to issues of relativism, ethical decision, and judgment.

67. Hennessey, *Materialist Feminism*, 15.

68. Ibid., 27.

69. Ibid., 97.

70. This term is used by Gustavo Gutiérrez in *A Theology of Liberation* (Maryknoll, N.Y.: Orbis Books, 1973), 10.

71. June Jordan, "Black Folks on Nicaragua: 'Leave Those Folks Alone!'" in *On Call: Political Essays* (Boston: South End Press, 1985), 59.

72. Delores S. Williams, "Womanist Theology: Black Women's Voices," in *Yearning to Breathe Free: Liberation Theologies in the U.S.*, ed. Mar Peter-Raoul, Linda Forcey, and Robert Hunter (Maryknoll, N.Y.: Orbis Books, 1990), 67.

73. Caraway, *Segregated Sisterhood*, 4.

74. Ibid., 119. See also Susan Thistlethwaite, *Sex, Race, and God: Christian Feminism in Black and White* (New York: Crossroad, 1989), chap. 2.

75. Caraway, *Segregated Sisterhood*, 166.

76. hooks, *Feminist Theory*, 44.

77. bell hooks, *Talking Back: Thinking Feminist, Thinking Black* (Boston: South End Press, 1989), 118.

78. hooks, *Yearning*, 110.

79. Kaye/Kantrowitz, *The Issue Is Power*, 129.

80. Ruth First, *117 days* (New York: Monthly Review Press, 1989), 8.

81. Kaye/Kantrowitz, *The Issue Is Power*, 113.

82. Barbara Smith, "Racism and Women's Studies," in *Making Face, Making Soul: Hacienda Caras: Creative and Critical Perspectives by Women of Color*, ed. Gloria Anzaldúa (San Francisco: Aunt Lute Foundation, 1990), 26.

83. hooks, *Feminist Theory*, 128; emphasis added.

84. See Sara Ruddick, *Maternal Thinking: Toward a Politics of Peace* (Boston: Beacon Press, 1989), for an attempt to move beyond this essentialized position.

85. Ibid., 137.

86. hooks, *Yearning*, 150–51.

87. Caraway, *Segregated Sisterhood*, 192.

88. Marsie Silvestro, "Crossing the Lines," in the album *Crossing the Lines* (privately recorded).

89. Caraway, *Segregated Sisterhood*, 201.

90. Lorde, "Age, Race, Class, and Sex," 115–16.

91. Ibid., 119.

92. Norma Alarcón, "The Theoretical Subject(s) of 'This Bridge Called My Back' and Anglo-American Feminism," in *Making Face*, 359.

93. Gloria Anzaldúa, introduction to *Making Face*, xxi.

94. See Anne Cameron, *Daughters of Copper Woman* (Vancouver, B.C.: Press Gang Publishers, 1981). Cameron was asked initially by the Nootka women themselves to write down and publish the stories that comprise the volume.

95. Anzaldúa, introduction to *Making Face*, xxi.

96. Hennessey, *Materialist Feminism*, 10.

97. Ibid., 11.

98. Audre Lorde, "The Master's Tools Will Never Dismantle the Master's House," in *Sister Outsider,* 110–11.

99. Beverly Harrison, "The Power of Anger in the Work of Love," in *Making the Connections: Essays in Feminist Social Ethics* (Boston: Beacon Press, 1985), 3–21.

100. Kaye/Kantrowitz, *The Issue Is Power,* 59.

101. Ibid., iii.

102. hooks, *Talking Back,* 179.

103. hooks, *Feminist Theory,* 63.

104. Marilyn James, "Continuing the Journey: Carrying Forward the Struggle," *Probe* 20, no. 3 (July/August, 1992): 4.

Chapter 6: Voices of Struggle, Echoes of God

1. Kathleen B. Jones, *Compassionate Authority: Democracy and the Representation of Women* (New York: Routledge, 1993), 161.

2. Onnie Lee Logan, *Motherwit: An Alabama Midwife's Story,* in collaboration with Kathryn Clark (New York: E. P. Hutton, 1989), 59.

3. Bettina Aptheker, *Tapestries of Life: Women's Work, Women's Consciousness, and the Meaning of Daily Experience* (Amherst: Univ. of Massachusetts Press, 1989), 173.

4. Jones, *Compassionate Authority,* 114.

5. Ibid., 119.

6. Rigoberta Menchú, *I, Rigoberta Menchú: An Indian Woman in Guatemala,* ed. Elisabeth Burgos-Debray; trans. Ann Wright (London: Verso, 1984), 228.

7. Chung Hyun Kyung, *Struggle to Be the Sun Again: Introducing Asian Women's Theology* (Maryknoll, N.Y.: Orbis Books, 1990), 103.

8. Donna J. Haraway, "The Promises of Monsters: A Regenerative Politics for Inappropriate/d Others," in *Cultural Studies,* ed. Lawrence Grossberg, Cary Nelson, and Paula A. Treichler (New York: Routledge, 1992), 295–337.

9. Haraway's work is highly suggestive of further possibilities for study and exploration of how other-than-human entities can be incorporated into such discourse in ways that do not replicate the distortions of representative practice.

10. Haraway, "Promise of Monsters," 311.

11. Ibid., 312.

12. See Joanne Carlson Brown and Carole R. Bohn, eds., *Christianity, Patriarchy, and Abuse: A Feminist Critique* (New York: Pilgrim Press, 1989), for a collection of feminist reflections on the role of the authoritarian Christian "Word" in perpetuating patterns of abuse and victimization and suppressing the agency and integrity of women.

13. See Madonna Kolbenschlag, ed., *Authority, Community and Conflict* (Kansas City: Sheed and Ward, 1986), for an exposition of the conflict between

the Vatican and the Sisters of Mercy over the holding of political office of three members of the Mercy community, and for a set of responses to the issues of authority and agency involved in that particular situation.

14. See Susan Cady, Marian Ronan, and Hal Taussig, *Sophia: The Future of Feminist Spirituality* (San Francisco: Harper and Row, 1986).

15. María Clara Bingemer, "Reflections on the Trinity," in *Through Her Eyes: Women's Theology from Latin America,* ed. Elsa Tamez (Maryknoll, N.Y.: Orbis Books, 1989), 61.

16. Ibid., 78.

17. Ibid., 79. Tom F. Driver, *Christ in a Changing World: Toward an Ethical Christology* (New York: Crossroad, 1981), 96–116, also suggests that trinitarian doctrine enables movement beyond dualism and into an *ethical* relativism that is concerned with "present reality in the context of infinite Spirit." See also Marjorie Hewitt Suchocki, *God Christ Church: A Practical Guide to Process Theology* (New York: Crossroad, 1986), for an understanding of the Trinity from a process theology perspective. Also, see Elizabeth A. Johnson, *She Who Is: The Mystery of God in Feminist Theological Discourse* (New York: Crossroad, 1992), chap. 10, for an exposition of the Trinity as presenting a utopian ideal of radical equality and mutuality for human relationships.

18. Donna J. Haraway, *Primate Visions: Gender, Race, and Nature in the World of Modern Science* (New York: Routledge, 1989), 378.

19. See chapter 3, above, for a more detailed exposition of the factors of exclusivity and essentialism in identity politics.

20. Carter Heyward, *The Redemption of God: A Theology of Mutual Relation* (Lanham, Md.: Univ. Press of America, 1982), 6. Heyward's book remains the most potentially useful theological rationale for a theo-ethic of articulation because of her refusal to deal simplistically with the reality of evil, particularly in imbalances of power. Thus the "right relations" of which Heyward speaks are no easy grace but are the hard-won result of struggle for justice. See also Carter Heyward, *Our Passion for Justice: Images of Power, Sexuality, and Liberation* (New York: Pilgrim Press, 1984).

21. I am indebted to Delores Williams and the students in "Spirituality and Politics in Cross-cultural Perspective," at Union Theological Seminary, spring 1993, for stimulating discussion around the issue of "privilege." For a helpful discussion of privilege, see also Peggy McIntosh, "White Privilege and Male Privilege: A Personal Account of Coming to See Correspondences through Work in Women's Studies," Working Paper No. 189 (Wellesley, Mass.: Center for Research on Women, 1988). McIntosh is particularly helpful in delineating the distinction between unearned privileges accruing simply because of skin color, sex, and so on, and "privileges" that *should* be available to all.

22. I use this form of the word "responsibility" to indicate its complex meaning. In my use of response/ability, I include not only the dimension of accountability but also that of empowerment through which one is *able* to *respond* to the complex oppressive structures that must be transformed.

Index